CW00347504

The 50 States Guide Book

by Vitalii Zaitcev

"Following the light of the sun, we left the Old World."
Christopher Columbus

Hello, dear reader!

Thank you for choosing our book! We promise you an unforgettable experience reading this atlas and exploring each state. We hope this book will inspire you to respect and explore the great outdoors. America has so much to offer; that's what inspired us to write this book and get our readers as amazed as we are with this vast and beautiful country. This map was designed both to tell a story and introduce you to all 50 states of America!

The 50 States Guide Book is much more than just another book of maps of the United States. This book was made to be something different: to be your guide to each state from the inside. We believe that every state has a story to tell, and we wanted those stories told all in one place.

Each state's section is packed with essential and curious information, such as history, current events, facts, trivia, beautiful illustrations, and close-up views of natural and cultural sites of great importance in every state. In addition, you will discover state flags and nicknames, state flowers and birds, and even fun and interesting laws! Each state's map also contains information about its neighbors, borders, and waters.

From sea to shining sea, from the arid West Texas to the icy glaciers in Alaska, America is one of the largest, most geographically diverse countries in the world. With world-class cities to boot, it's worth exploring every corner of this great nation. Take a browse through the book and learn about all of them!

We're sure you'll enjoy reading through our overview of every state, and we had so much fun preparing it for you. Plus, at the end of the book, you will find a gallery of the Presidents of the United States from its foundation to the present day, with dates of presidencies and names! We added this historical bonus just to make our book even more informative and interesting.

So, what are you waiting for? Let your journey begin!

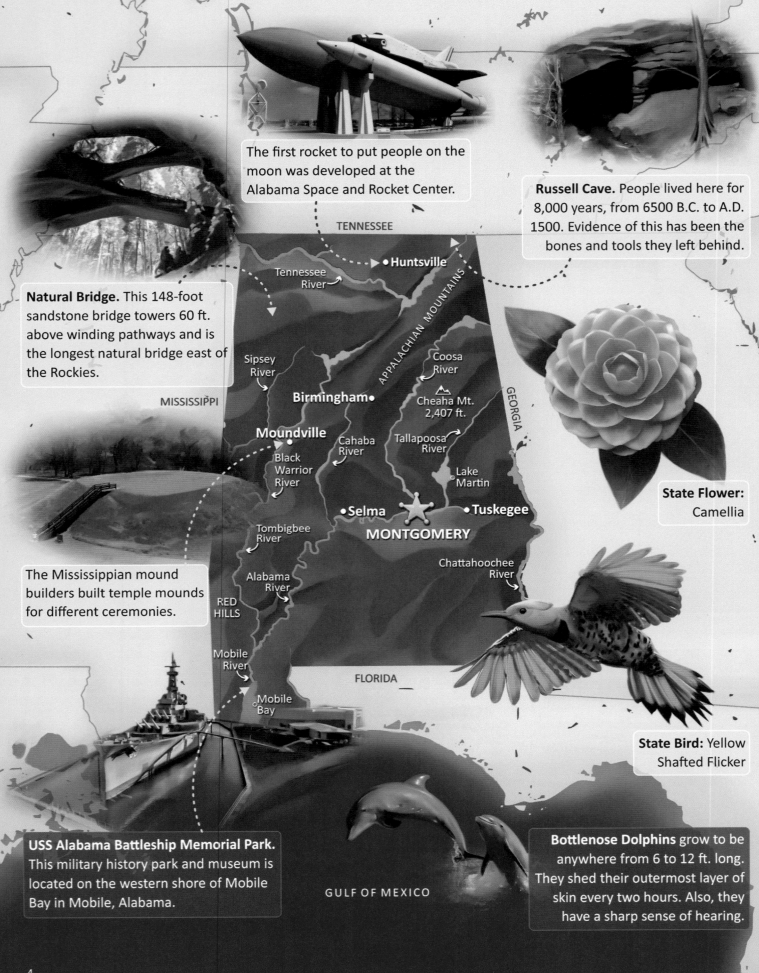

The first rocket to put people on the moon was developed at the Alabama Space and Rocket Center.

Russell Cave. People lived here for 8,000 years, from 6500 B.C. to A.D. 1500. Evidence of this has been the bones and tools they left behind.

Natural Bridge. This 148-foot sandstone bridge towers 60 ft. above winding pathways and is the longest natural bridge east of the Rockies.

The Mississippian mound builders built temple mounds for different ceremonies.

State Flower: Camellia

State Bird: Yellow Shafted Flicker

USS Alabama Battleship Memorial Park. This military history park and museum is located on the western shore of Mobile Bay in Mobile, Alabama.

Bottlenose Dolphins grow to be anywhere from 6 to 12 ft. long. They shed their outermost layer of skin every two hours. Also, they have a sharp sense of hearing.

TENNESSEE

MISSISSIPPI

GEORGIA

FLORIDA

GULF OF MEXICO

Tennessee River

Huntsville

APPALACHIAN MOUNTAINS

Sipsey River

Coosa River

Cheaha Mt. 2,407 ft.

Birmingham

Moundville

Cahaba River

Tallapoosa River

Black Warrior River

Lake Martin

Selma

Tuskegee

MONTGOMERY

Tombigbee River

Chattahoochee River

Alabama River

RED HILLS

Mobile River

Mobile Bay

4

ALABAMA/AL

WELCOME TO THE HEART OF DIXIE

The Basics:
Total area: 52,420 sq. mi (135,767 sq. km)
Land area: 50,545 sq. mi (131,171 sq. km)
Population: 4,874,700
Capital: Montgomery

STORY TO KNOW

The history of Alabama is long, conflicted, and colorful. The first European settlers were French, but battles between them, the Native Americans, and the English were ongoing for hundreds of years. After becoming the 22nd state, Alabama then seceded during the Civil War, and its capital Montgomery, was the Southern capital during those years. The Civil Rights movement also found its home in this state, with both Martin Luther King Jr. and Rosa Parks hailing from and organizing their movements in Alabama.

The economy has struggled in post-conflict periods, but NASA calls much of the state home for its construction and engineering facilities, and in 2002, Asian automakers opened plants in the state which provided thousands of jobs. It's also famous for its soul food, colonial architecture, college football rivalries, and the many famous musicians, politicians, and athletes who have called Alabama home. From Mobile to Montgomery, and everything in between and all around, there are plenty of places to see and things to do.

The State Motto: "WE DARE MOUNTAINS OUR RIGHTS"

The Facts:
Alabama became the 22nd state on December 14, 1819.
Major cities: Birmingham, Montgomery, Mobile, Huntsville, Tuscaloosa
Border states: Florida, Georgia, Mississippi, Tennessee

How Alabama got its name:
The name Alabama comes from a Native American tribe that lived in the middle of the state. They named the local river the Alabama River, and the state took its name from this river.

Fun Laws:
• You may not have an ice cream cone in your back pocket at any time!
• Bear wrestling matches are prohibited.

Good to know!
• Montgomery, Al was the capital of the Confederate States.
• The first electric trolley was introduced in Montgomery in 1886.
• The world's largest cast iron statue, called The Vulcan, is in Birmingham. It is 56 ft. tall!

The Aurora Borealis.
The bright dancing lights of the aurora are actually collisions between electrically charged particles from the sun entering the earth's atmosphere. The lights are seen above the magnetic poles of the northern and southern hemispheres.

The Arctic National Wildlife Refuge is home to all three species of North American bear: polar, black, and grizzly.

State Flower: Forget-me-not

ARCTIC OCEAN

Point Barrow Northernmost point in U. S. A.

Do you believe in Santa? If not, a visit to North Pole, Alaska is in order. This community of 2,200 residents keeps the Christmas spirit alive all year long.

CANADA

BROOKS RANGE

BERING STRAIT

Glaciers, earthquakes, and ocean storms have shaped Alaska's Kenai Fjords for centuries, resulting in rugged landscapes and constantly changing terrain.

Kotzebue

ARCTIC CIRCLE

FortYukon

Circle

Fairbanks

North Pole

Denali: Highest peak in N.A. 20,320 ft.

YukonRiver

Nome

Wrangel St.Elias Mts.

State Bird: Willow Ptarmigan

ALASKA RANGE

Anchorage

Valdez

JUNEAU

Seward

Bethel

GULF OF ALASKA

Humpback whales are enormous creatures — about the size of a school bus. They are known for their haunting and melodic songs and for breaching the water with amazing acrobatic abilities.

PACIFIC OCEAN

Aleutian Islands

At approximately 17 million acres, **the Tongass National Forest** is America's largest national forest. It's roughly the size of West Virginia!

The Kodiak bear is a subspecies of the brown or grizzly bear. They are the world's largest, standing 10 ft. tall or more on their hind legs.

ALASKA /AK

WELCOME TO THE LAST FRONTIER

The Basics:
Total area: 665,384 sq. mi (1,723,337 sq. km)
Land area: 570,641 sq. mi (1,477,953 sq. km)
Population: 739,795
Capital: Juneau

STORY TO KNOW

Alaska, the nation's largest state, was also the second-to-last to join the country. The land was first purchased from Russia in 1867 for only two cents an acre – even that was considered a bad deal at first, but soon, gold was discovered, and later, oil. The region has astronomically exceeded its initial cost in return on investment, and today it is a much-beloved state in America. It is home to the highest mountain in North America, Denali (previously known as Mt. McKinley), and it has also suffered the most severe earthquake in American history: a 9.2 magnitude in 1964, which scarred the coastline and whose impacts are still visible today.

The territory was first settled over 10,000 years ago, likely by travelers who crossed the Bering Land Bridge from Siberia. These are today the Aleut people, and many of their traditions are still present in Alaska. From skinning and tanning their own animal hides, to traditional fishing practices, these customs have persisted through millennia and are part of Alaskan heritage. The state is also famous for the Iditarod: a dog sled trail race covering nearly 2,500 miles of land, known and competed in by people from around the world. The solitary landscapes, pristine natural beauty, and rugged individualism of Alaska have come to represent a distinct and unique corner of American life that can only be understood by immersing oneself in it.

The State Motto: "NORTH TO THE FUTURE"

The Facts: 🤓
Alaska became the 49th state on January 3, 1959.
Major cities: Anchorage, Fairbanks, Juneau, Badger
Borders: Canada, the Gulf of Alaska, the Pacific Ocean, The Bering Sea, and the Arctic Ocean

How Alaska got its name: 😃
The word Alaska comes from the Aleut word "Alaxsxaq," which means "the Mainland."

Fun Laws: 🙂
• While it is legal to shoot bears, waking a sleeping bear for the purpose of taking a photograph is prohibited.

Good to know! 💡
• The capital of Alaska, Juneau, does not connect with the rest of Alaska (or any portion of the United States) by land. You can only get there by boat or plane.
• Alaska is the largest U.S. state, by far. Its twice as big as the next largest state, Texas.
(Almost 1/5 as large as the rest of the USA).
• Gold was discovered here in 1896.

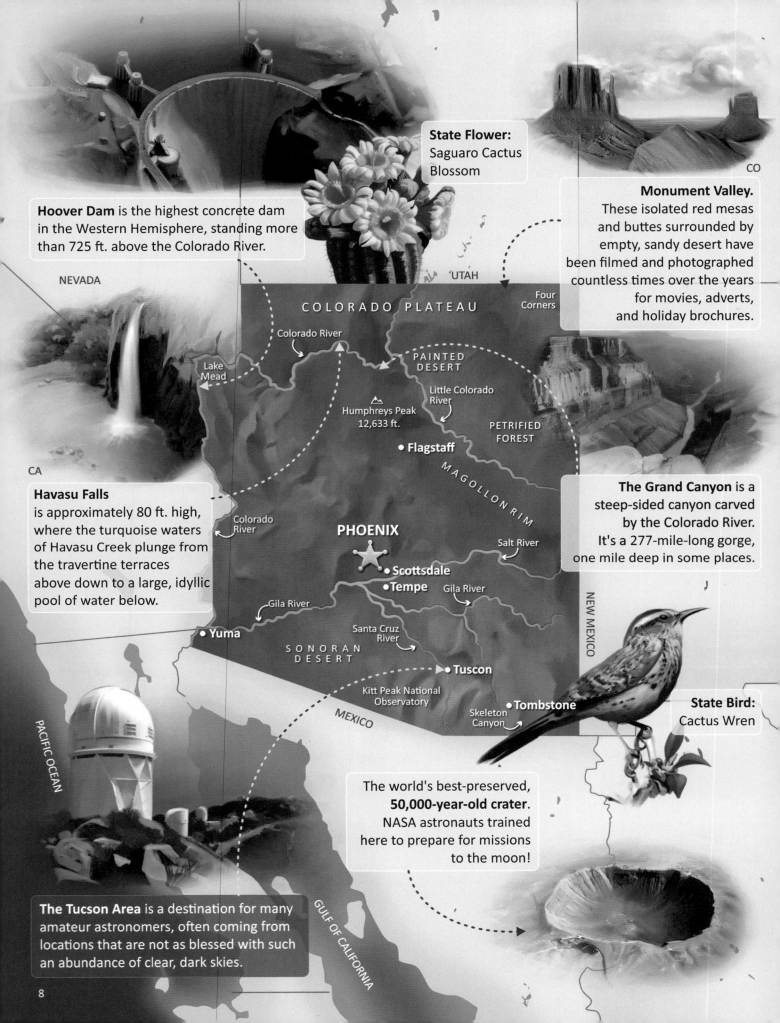

State Flower: Saguaro Cactus Blossom

Hoover Dam is the highest concrete dam in the Western Hemisphere, standing more than 725 ft. above the Colorado River.

Monument Valley. These isolated red mesas and buttes surrounded by empty, sandy desert have been filmed and photographed countless times over the years for movies, adverts, and holiday brochures.

NEVADA

UTAH

CO

COLORADO PLATEAU

Four Corners

Colorado River

Lake Mead

PAINTED DESERT

Little Colorado River

△ Humphreys Peak 12,633 ft.

PETRIFIED FOREST

CA

Havasu Falls is approximately 80 ft. high, where the turquoise waters of Havasu Creek plunge from the travertine terraces above down to a large, idyllic pool of water below.

Colorado River

● Flagstaff

MAGOLLON RIM

PHOENIX

Salt River

● Scottsdale

● Tempe

Gila River

The Grand Canyon is a steep-sided canyon carved by the Colorado River. It's a 277-mile-long gorge, one mile deep in some places.

Gila River

● Yuma

SONORAN DESERT

Santa Cruz River

● Tuscon

Kitt Peak National Observatory

MEXICO

Skeleton Canyon

● Tombstone

NEW MEXICO

State Bird: Cactus Wren

PACIFIC OCEAN

The world's best-preserved, **50,000-year-old crater.** NASA astronauts trained here to prepare for missions to the moon!

The Tucson Area is a destination for many amateur astronomers, often coming from locations that are not as blessed with such an abundance of clear, dark skies.

GULF OF CALIFORNIA

ARIZONA / AZ

WELCOME TO THE GRAND CANYON STATE

The Basics:
Total area: 113,990 sq. mi (295,234 sq. km)
Land area: 113,594 sq. mi (294,207 sq. km)
Population: 7,016,300
Capital: Phoenix

STORY TO KNOW

Arizona was the last of the continental United States to join the union, becoming a state only in 1912. After being first visited by the Spanish in the 1500s, it took three centuries of clashing between Spanish and American settlers and the Native Americans in the area before it became the state it is today. It was home to Apache warriors like Cochise and Geronimo, and lawless towns like Tombstone play a large role in our modern glamorizing of the wild west. Back then, and through to today, much of Arizona's economy has been based on what are called the 5 Cs: copper, cattle, cotton, citrus, and climate. In modern times, manufacturing and service have also arisen in the state.

Without a doubt, Arizona's most famous landmark has got to be the Grand Canyon. Known around the world, this spectacular 277-mile-long gorge is carved out by the Colorado River, and its beauty is said to be unparalleled anywhere. This unforgiving desert has far more than just the Grand Canyon to offer, however: Monument Valley and the sunset glow of Cathedral Rock are nearly as magnificent in themselves. The state's cities are rapidly growing, from Phoenix to Tucson to Bisbee, and while the Sonoran Desert may not seem like a hospitable place, you wouldn't know it from the thriving communities in these urban settlements. Creativity from the arts to the cuisine abound here, so don't miss a visit – you may even decide to stay!

The State Motto: "GOD ENRICHES"

The Facts: 🤓
Arizona became the 48th state on February 14, 1912.
Major cities: Phoenix, Tucson, Mesa, Chandler, Glendale, Scottsdale, Gilbert
Border states: California, Colorado, Nevada, New Mexico

How Arizona got its name: 🙂
Historians are not sure exactly where the name for Arizona originated. Most think that it came from a Native American word meaning "Little spring." Some other names were considered for the territory, including Montezuma and Arizuma.

Fun Laws: 😶
• There is a possible 25 years in prison for cutting down a cactus.

Good to know! 💡
• Arizona is home to the Gila Monster, the only poisonous lizard in the United States.
• Arizona's geography varies from hot deserts to high snowy mountains.

TOAD SUCK DAZE 2018 · CONWAY, ARKANSAS

Toad Suck is an annual toad race. Each year, during the first weekend in May, more than 100,000 people gather in the streets of downtown Conway for Toad Suck Daze.

Blanchard Spring Caverns is one of the most spectacular and carefully-developed caves found anywhere in the world. The caverns contain caves as long as four football fields.

State Bird: Mockingbird

State gem: Diamond. Crater of Diamonds State Park is the only diamond-producing site in the USA where the public can search for diamonds.

Popeye Statue is a giant bronze sculpture in the city of Alma which claims to be the "Spinach Capital of the World."

Lake Ouachita is one of the cleanest lakes in the USA. Also, it's home to rare freshwater jellyfish.

State Flower: Apple blossom

MISSOURI

OZARK PLATEAU

BOSTON MOUNTAINS

• Fayetteville

Strawberry River

Black River

Blanchard Springs Caverns

Jonesboro •

• Fort Smith

Magazine Mountain 2,753 ft.

OUACHITA MOUNTAINS

St. Francis River

White River

LITTLE ROCK

Like Ouachita

• Hot Springs

Arkansas River

TENNESSEE

MISSISSIPPI

OKLAHOMA

Red River

• Hope

Ouachita River

Mississippi River

TEXAS

• Texarkana

LOUISIANA

ARKANSAS/AR

WELCOME TO THE NATURAL STATE

The Basics:
Total area: 53,179 sq. mi (137,732 sq. km)
Land area: 25,035 sq. mi (134,771 sq. km)
Population: 3,004,300
Capital: Little Rock

STORY TO KNOW

Arkansas is a state steeped in history and natural beauty alike. It fell under American control with the Louisiana Purchase in 1803, and it then became the 25th state in 1836. It shortly joined the Confederacy during the Civil War in 1861. Unfortunately, Arkansas fell on hard times following the South's defeat, and it took many years before its agriculture began to pick up again. Now, it produces rice, poultry, and grain, and it has a booming oil and gas sector. It's also home to the Walmart headquarters. Of further historical significance was the all-white Central High School in Little Rock, where nine African-American youths attended in 1957 – a watershed moment in the Civil Rights movement.

The state is home to the Ozarks, the Ouachita Mountains, Crater of Diamonds State Park, and world-famous hot springs. There are rivers, lakes, forests, and everything in between! You can even visit the Crater of Diamonds and dig for your own – their "finders keepers" policy means you might be able to strike it rich if you find any of the glittering diamonds during your hunt. While many do not think of Arkansas for its landscapes, it is called the "Natural State" for a good reason!

The State Motto: "THE PEOPLE RULE"

The Facts: 🤓
Arkansas became the 25th state on June 15, 1836.
Major cities: Little Rock, Fort Smith, Fayetteville, Springdale, Jonesboro
Border states: Louisiana, Texas, Oklahoma, Missouri, Mississippi, Tennessee

How Arkansas got its name: 🤭
The name Arkansas comes from the Native American Quapaw word "Akakaze," which means "Land of the downriver people."

Fun Laws: 😂
• It's strictly prohibited to pronounce "Arkansas" incorrectly.

Good to know! 💡
• The state flag has 25 stars on it to symbolize Arkansas becoming the 25th state.
• The state is known for its beautiful lakes, rivers, and hot springs. It has over 600,000 acres of lakes.

The federal prison on Alcatraz Island in the chilly waters of California's San Francisco Bay housed some of America's most difficult and dangerous felons, included gangster Al Capone, during its years of operation from 1934 to 1963.

OREGON

State Flower: Golden Poppy

Silicon Valley is home to the top tech companies in the world located in San Francisco Bay Area.

PACIFIC OCEAN

SIERRA NEVADA MOUNTAINS

Sacramento River

COAST RANGE

SACRAMENTO

NEVADA

Lake Tahoe

The Golden Gate Bridge is a suspension bridge connecting San Francisco to California's northern counties. With its tremendous 746-foot tall towers, sweeping main cables, and one-mile width, it's quite a spectacle.

San Francisco

Oakland

San Jose

Sequoia National Park

Mt. Whitney 14,495 ft.

The Fallen Tunnel Log of Sequoia National Park came into being after an unnamed giant sequoia fell across the Crescent Meadow Road.

San Joaquin River

DEATH VALLEY

COAST RANGE

MOJAVE DESERT

HOLLYWOOD

The Hollywood Sign is an American landmark and cultural icon located in Los Angeles, standing 45 ft. tall.

Los Angeles

Colorado River   ARIZONA

Death Valley. This is North America's driest and hottest spot and has the lowest elevation on the continent —282 ft. below sea level.

San Diego

MEXICO

GULF OF CALIFORNIA

State Bird: California Quail

Disneyland is the place where the stories of Disney, Pixar, and more come to life!

CALIFORNIA/CA

 WELCOME TO THE GOLDEN STATE

The Basics:
Total area: 163,695 sq. mi (423,967 sq. km)
Land area: 155,779 sq. mi (403,466 sq. km)
Population: 39,536,700
Capital: Sacramento

STORY TO KNOW

California has more people than any other state in the USA! It was first colonized in 1769, but it didn't actually join the United States until 1847, after a war with Mexico. Soon after, gold was discovered at Sutter's Mill, and the gold rush began. People from all over the country and around the world began heading to California to make their fortunes in gold, and many of them settled there and built the state into what it is today – a hub for agriculture, high-tech industry, manufacturing, entertainment, and much more!

Today, the state has an economy that rivals some of the largest nations in the world, and visitors are attracted to all that it has to offer. Explorers and can enjoy its many famous attractions: from Disneyland to Yosemite, there is truly something for everyone. The famous Golden Gate Bridge in the City by the Bay (San Francisco) and the Hollywood Walk of Fame in the City of Angels (Los Angeles) are just a few of California's world-renowned attractions, but with millions of acres of state and national parks, including Yosemite, Joshua Tree, and the Redwoods, you don't have to go to the cities to enjoy yourself!

The State Motto: "EUREKA"

The Facts: 😎
California became the 31st state on September 9, 1850.
Major cities: Los Angeles, San Diego, San Jose, San Francisco, Fresno, Sacramento
Border states: Arizona, Nevada, Oregon

How California got its name: 😃
California was named by Spanish explorers who thought they had discovered an island. The name comes from the Spanish story of Queen Califia who ruled a mythical island.

Fun Laws: 😄 😃
• Sunshine is guaranteed to the masses.

Good to know! 💡
• California is home to the highest point (Mt. Whitney) and the lowest point (Death Valley) in the continental United States.
• It was 134°F (57°C) in Death Valley in July 1913, the highest temperature ever recorded in the USA.
• The first McDonald's restaurant was opened in San Bernardino, California in 1940.

State Flower:
Rocky Mountain Columbine

Glenwood Hot Springs
is the world's largest
hot springs pool.

The Colorado Mountains
are the best for skiing and
snowboarding nearly
anywhere in the world!

Sandboarding
is an extreme board
sport which takes
place on sand dunes
similar to snowboarding
and iceboarding.

WYOMING

NEBRASKA

ROCKY MOUNTAINS

Continental
Divide

●Fort Collins
●Greeley

South Platte River

●Boulder

DENVER

Vail ●

Colorado River

KANSAS

Denver, the
Mile High City,
is 5,280 feet
above sea level.

Aspen ●

Mt. Elbert
14,433 ft.

Colorado Springs ●

Gunnison
River

Pikes Peak

Dolores
River

●**Pueblo**

Arkansas River

State Bird:
Lark Bunting

Rio Grande

San Juan
River

UTAH

●**Mesa Verde**

ARIZONA

NEW MEXICO

OKLAHOMA

Four Corners Monument
is the only place in the
United States where four
states intersect.

Garden of the Gods
is the top geological
wonder in Colorado,
with incredible rock
formations and
amazing view.

Ancient Anasazi.
The cliff dwellings of Mesa
Verde are some of the most
notable and best preserved
on the North American
continent.

COLORADO /CO

WELCOME TO THE MOTHER OF RIVERS STATE

The Basics:
Total area: 104,094 sq. mi (269,601 sq. km)
Land area: 103,642 sq. mi (268,431 sq. km)
Population: 5,607,200
Capital: Denver

STORY TO KNOW

Described by many as "God's Own Country," Colorado, it is argued, is the nation's most beautiful state. The soaring Rocky Mountains are perhaps most aptly captured by Katharine Lee Bates, who wrote her song "America the Beautiful" after experiencing the breathtaking vistas of Pikes Peak, one of Colorado's highest points. At the base of these magnificent pinnacles lie grassland prairies, with all these regions providing a home to elk, moose, and bighorn sheep. The mountains also rest on mineral deposits including silver and gold, which gave rise to much of the prospectors' push west in the 1800s.

The Native Americans of Colorado were both cliff-dwelling and plains-dwelling people. After Eastern Colorado became part of U.S. territory with the Louisiana Purchase, and once gold was discovered, conflict began to arise with these original inhabitants, include the Cheyenne and Arapaho peoples. As in other cases, the settlers were the victorious ones, and the eventual completion of the transcontinental railroad made the settlements permanent. Today, the industry of these prospectors and miners is still present, but agriculture, energy, tourism, and other budding new industries have largely taken over.

The State Motto: "NOTHING WITHOUT PROVIDENCE"

The Facts: 🤓
Colorado became the 38th state on August 1, 1876.
Major cities: Denver, Colorado Springs, Aurora, Fort Collins, Lakewood, Thornton
Border states: Kansas, Nebraska, Wyoming, Utah, Arizona, New Mexico, Oklahoma

How Colorado got its name: 🤪
Colorado comes from a Spanish word meaning "Red-colored." It is named for the red mud of the Colorado River.

Fun Laws: 😄
• One may not mutilate a rock in a state park.

Good to know! 💡
• The capital of Colorado, Denver, is almost exactly 1 mile above sea level. This is how it earned the nickname 'Mile High City'.
• The highest city in the United States is Leadville. It is 10,430 ft. above sea level.

The Helicopter - was invented in Connecticut in 1939 by Igor Sikorsky.

The first American Dictionary was written by Noah Webster (1758-1843), who was a journalist and teacher in Connecticut.

State Flower: Mountain Laurel

The Praying Mantis is a state insect. It can be green or brown, and it eats aphids, flies, grasshoppers, caterpillars, and moths.

State Bird: Robin

MASSACHUSETTS

🔺 Mt. Frissell 2,380 ft.

TACONIC MOUNTAINS

NEW YORK

RHODE ISLAND

• Falls Village

Willimantic River

Quinebang River

HARTFORD

Litchfield •

○ Bantam Lake

Shepaug River

Rocky Hill •

Shetucket River

Waterbury

Naugatuck River

Connecticut River

Thames River

○ Lake Candlewood

Quinnipiac River

New London

• **Groton**

Housatonic River

New Haven

Bridgeport •

USS Nautilus - The first nuclear submarine was launched from Groton Submarine Base here in 1954.

Norwalk •

Stamford •

LONG ISLAND SOUND

Foxwoods is the largest casino resort in the world, covering an area of 9,000,000 sq. ft.

ATLANTIC OCEAN

CONNECTICUT/CT

WELCOME TO THE CONSTITUTION STATE

The Basics:
Total area: 5,543 sq. mi (14,542 sq. km)
Land area: 4,842 sq. mi (12,542 sq. km)
Population: 3,588,200
Capital: Hartford

STORY TO KNOW

Connecticut was first colonized in the early 1600s, making it one of the first states in America to be settled by Europeans. These early settlers played an important role in the American Revolution, and its government was a model for the U. S. constitution, earning it the nickname the "Constitution State." As true then as it is today, Connecticut is an industrial powerhouse, producing everything from jet engines to military goods. In addition, the state is today home to a large portion of the American insurance industry.

Although Connecticut is small in size, it is densely populated (among the most densely populated in the country!), and this has led to its outperforming of other larger states in terms of the notable people it produces. From revolutionary war hero Nathan Hale to inventor Charles Goodyear to author Suzanne Collins (of *The Hunger Games*), Connecticut has a proud heritage of industrious, bold, and creative citizens. As the fifth state in the Union, it boasts numerous firsts: first law school, first public art museum, first pay phone, and more! Even today, it continues leading the charge well above its weight class.

The State Motto: "HE WHO TRANSPLANTED STILL SUSTAINS"

The Facts: 🤓
Connecticut became the 5th state on January 9, 1788.
Major cities: Bridgeport, New Haven, Hartford, Stamford, Waterbury
Border states: Rhode Island, Massachusetts, New York

How Connecticut got its name: 🤪
The name Connecticut comes from the Native American Algonquian word "Quonehtacut," which means "Land of the long river."

Fun Laws: 😄
• In order for a pickle to officially be considered a pickle, it must bounce.

Good to know! 💡
• This state is the home to many inventions including the helicopter, sewing machine, vulcanized rubber (for tires), revolver, and the cotton gin.
• In 1901, the first law regarding automobiles was passed. It set the speed limit at 12 miles per hour. Don't drive too fast!

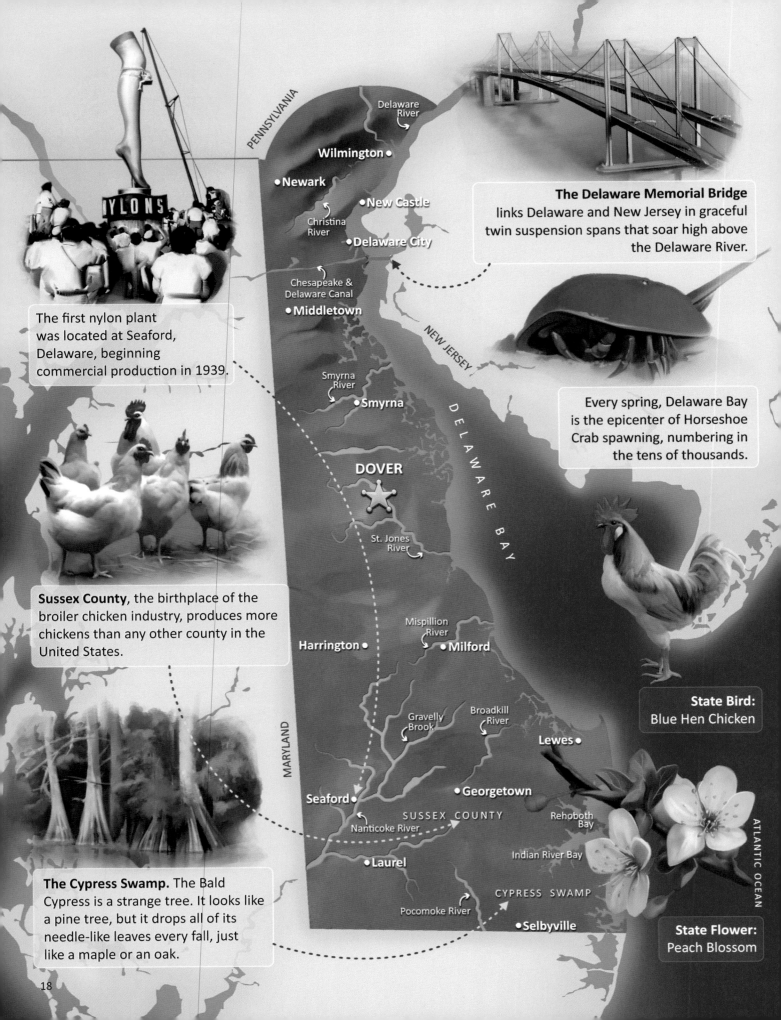

The first nylon plant was located at Seaford, Delaware, beginning commercial production in 1939.

Sussex County, the birthplace of the broiler chicken industry, produces more chickens than any other county in the United States.

The Cypress Swamp. The Bald Cypress is a strange tree. It looks like a pine tree, but it drops all of its needle-like leaves every fall, just like a maple or an oak.

The Delaware Memorial Bridge links Delaware and New Jersey in graceful twin suspension spans that soar high above the Delaware River.

Every spring, Delaware Bay is the epicenter of Horseshoe Crab spawning, numbering in the tens of thousands.

State Bird: Blue Hen Chicken

State Flower: Peach Blossom

PENNSYLVANIA

Delaware River

Wilmington

Newark

New Castle

Christina River

Delaware City

Chesapeake & Delaware Canal

Middletown

NEW JERSEY

Smyrna River

Smyrna

DELAWARE BAY

DOVER

St. Jones River

Harrington

Mispillion River

Milford

MARYLAND

Gravelly Brook

Broadkill River

Lewes

Seaford

Georgetown

SUSSEX COUNTY

Rehoboth Bay

Nanticoke River

Indian River Bay

Laurel

CYPRESS SWAMP

Pocomoke River

Selbyville

ATLANTIC OCEAN

DELAWARE/DE

WELCOME TO THE FIRST STATE

The Basics:
Total area: 2,489 sq. mi (6,446 sq. km)
Land area: 1,949 sq. mi (5,047 sq. km)
Population: 961,939
Capital: Dover

STORY TO KNOW

Delaware may be the second smallest state in the country, but its historical impact outweighs that of many of its larger counterparts. The Delaware River Valley was one of the earliest settled regions on the Eastern seaboard, and it was the first state to ratify the United States constitution in 1787. Its significance remains even today, as it is home not only to popular Atlantic beaches for tourists and residents alike, but also to significant agricultural and industrial output – from soybeans and dairy to machinery and chemical products. The crossover between these industries has made for a healthy concern for the environment within the state.

This "Small Wonder" state was first settled by Europeans in 1638, but Delaware was home to the Lenni Lenape ("Original People") tribe long before this. For thousands of years, these indigenous people made the Delaware River their home, and some still remain today. They now share what little remains with colonial settlers, hunting, fishing, and farming alongside them. Other interesting features of Delaware include its sandy beaches, cypress swamps, and the DuPont Experimental Station. It's also home to the inventors of nylon and Gore-Tex!

The State Motto: "LIBERTY AND INDEPENDENCE"

The Facts:
Delaware became the 1st state on December 7, 1787.
Major cities: Wilmington, Dover, Newark, Middletown
Border states: New Jersey, Pennsylvania, Maryland

How Delaware got its name:
The state was named after a governor of Virginia named Lord De La Warr.

Fun Laws:
• It is illegal to fly over any body of water, unless one is carrying sufficient supplies of food and drink.

Good to know!
• Delaware is called the 'First State' because it was the first state to join the Union.
• Delaware is only 35 miles across at its widest point. It is the second smallest US state.

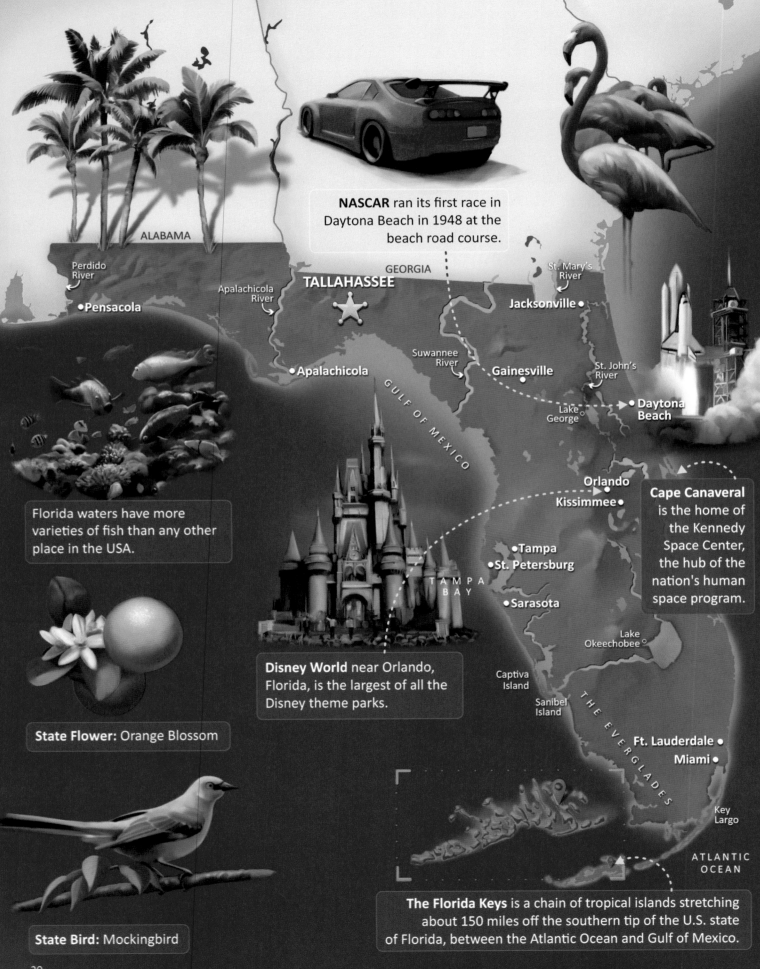

NASCAR ran its first race in Daytona Beach in 1948 at the beach road course.

ALABAMA

Perdido River

•**Pensacola**

Apalachicola River

GEORGIA

TALLAHASSEE

St. Mary's River

Jacksonville •

•**Apalachicola**

Suwannee River

Gainesville

St. John's River

GULF OF MEXICO

Lake George

•**Daytona Beach**

Florida waters have more varieties of fish than any other place in the USA.

Orlando
Kissimmee•

Cape Canaveral is the home of the Kennedy Space Center, the hub of the nation's human space program.

•**Tampa**
•**St. Petersburg**

TAMPA BAY

•**Sarasota**

Lake Okeechobee ○

Disney World near Orlando, Florida, is the largest of all the Disney theme parks.

Captiva Island

Sanibel Island

THE EVERGLADES

Ft. Lauderdale •

Miami •

State Flower: Orange Blossom

Key Largo

ATLANTIC OCEAN

State Bird: Mockingbird

The Florida Keys is a chain of tropical islands stretching about 150 miles off the southern tip of the U.S. state of Florida, between the Atlantic Ocean and Gulf of Mexico.

FLORIDA / FL

WELCOME TO THE TROPICAL STATE

The Basics:
Total area: 65,758 sq. mi (170,312 sq. km)
Land area: 53,625 sq. mi (138,887 sq. km)
Population: 20,984,400
Capital: Tallahassee

STORY TO KNOW

Florida was the first state in the nation to be permanently settled by Europeans, in 1565. The Spanish founded St. Augustine that year, and in the following centuries, the state would be a hotbed for conflict, with numerous wars over control of the land against Native Americans and then again during the Civil War. It became a state in 1845, and to this day it remains one of the most diverse states in the country, with a significant Latin American and African-American population.

The climate attracts retirees and tourists alike from all over the country and even the world. Florida is home to orange farmers, athletes, golfers, and Mickey Mouse. From Orlando to Miami to the Florida Keys, there is something for everyone in the Sunshine State. However, managing such a large state with so many varying economies and interests is no easy task. Regional and federal governments must constantly be balancing the interests of Florida's many urban citizens with its rural farmers, while at the same time ensuring tourism isn't hurt and the critically important natural environments are not damaged.

The State Motto: "IN GOD WE TRUST"

The Facts: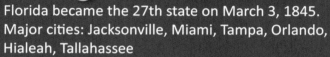
Florida became the 27th state on March 3, 1845.
Major cities: Jacksonville, Miami, Tampa, Orlando, Hialeah, Tallahassee
Border states: Alabama, Georgia

How Florida got its name: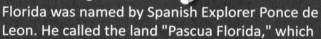
Florida was named by Spanish Explorer Ponce de Leon. He called the land "Pascua Florida," which means "Flowery Easter."

Fun Laws:
• The state constitution allows for freedom of speech, a trial by jury, and pregnant pigs to not be confined in cages.

Good to know!
• St. Augustine, Florida was founded in 1565 and is the oldest permanent city in the United States.
• Florida is sometimes called the Alligator State because of all the alligators that live there. Also, the University of Florida's mascot is the Gator. This is where Gatorade was first invented.
• Florida grows 80% of the nation's oranges and grapefruits.

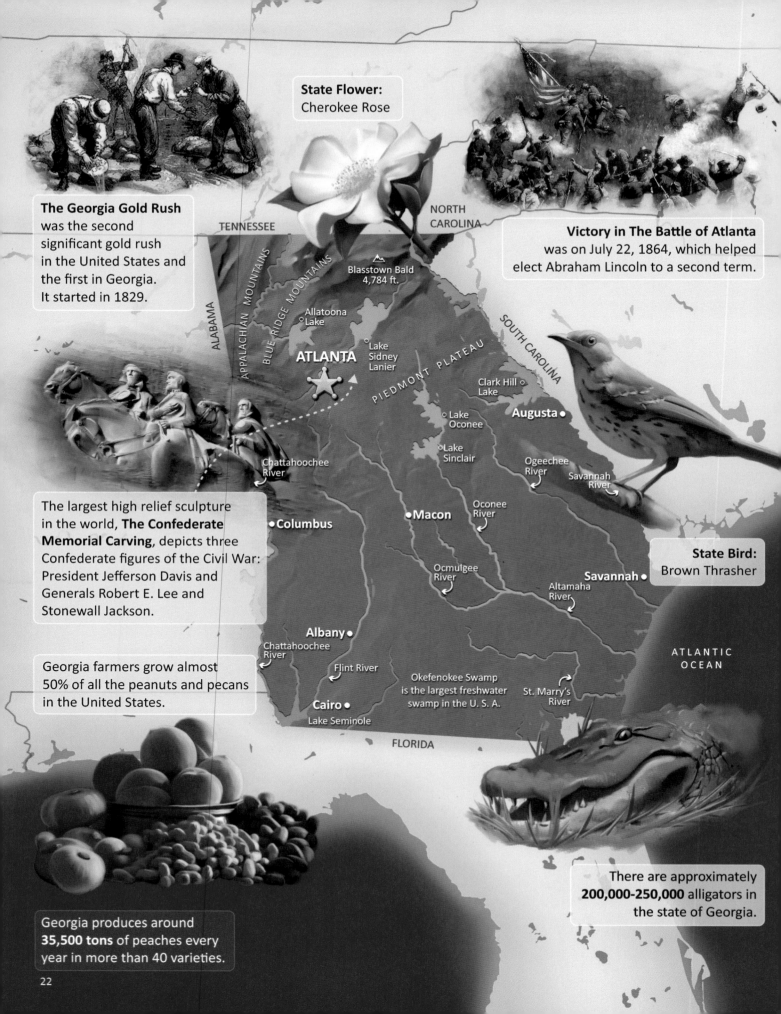

State Flower:
Cherokee Rose

The Georgia Gold Rush
was the second
significant gold rush
in the United States and
the first in Georgia.
It started in 1829.

Victory in The Battle of Atlanta
was on July 22, 1864, which helped
elect Abraham Lincoln to a second term.

TENNESSEE

NORTH CAROLINA

ALABAMA

APPALACHIAN MOUNTAINS

BLUE RIDGE MOUNTAINS

Blasstown Bald
4,784 ft.

Allatoona
Lake

ATLANTA

Lake
Sidney
Lanier

PIEDMONT PLATEAU

SOUTH CAROLINA

Clark Hill
Lake

Lake
Oconee

Augusta

Lake
Sinclair

Chattahoochee
River

Ogeechee
River

Savannah
River

The largest high relief sculpture
in the world, **The Confederate
Memorial Carving**, depicts three
Confederate figures of the Civil War:
President Jefferson Davis and
Generals Robert E. Lee and
Stonewall Jackson.

•**Columbus**

•**Macon**

Oconee
River

Ocmulgee
River

Savannah•

Altamaha
River

State Bird:
Brown Thrasher

Albany•

Chattahoochee
River

Flint River

Okefenokee Swamp
is the largest freshwater
swamp in the U. S. A.

St. Marry's
River

ATLANTIC
OCEAN

Georgia farmers grow almost
50% of all the peanuts and pecans
in the United States.

Cairo •

Lake Seminole

FLORIDA

Georgia produces around
35,500 tons of peaches every
year in more than 40 varieties.

There are approximately
200,000-250,000 alligators in
the state of Georgia.

GEORGIA/GA

WELCOME TO THE EMPIRE STATE OF SOUTH

The Basics:
Total area: 59,425 sq. mi (153,910 sq. km)
Land area: 57,513 sq. mi (148,959 sq. km)
Population: 10,429,400
Capital: Atlanta

STORY TO KNOW

The land now known as Georgia was inhabited for thousands of years by Cherokee, Cree, and other Native tribes until the mid-1500s, when the first European settlements began to spring up. The first colony to really take hold was founded in 1733 by James Oglethorpe, in present-day Savannah. In these early days, agriculture and slavery were the primary economic factors in the state, and this was true until the defeat of the South in the Civil War. Georgia fell on hard times after this, but in modern years has re-emerged as a cultural and economic landmark in America.

The beaches, history, and climate in Georgia draw visitors from all over the country. It's also got a thriving music scene, having been home to Gladys Knight, CeeLo Green, and of course Ray Charles. The so-called Peach State has plenty to offer even the most avid outdoorsmen, too: from the Blue Ridge Mountains to the Appalachian Trail, and from a tour through historic Savannah to a stroll in rural countryside. The hospitality, charm, and comfort of Georgia make it one of the most pleasurable states south of the Mason Dixon line to visit or live.

The State Motto: "WISDOM, JUSTICE AND MODERATION"

The Facts:
Georgia became the 4th state on January 2, 1788.
Major cities: Atlanta, Augusta, Columbus, Savannah, Athens
Border states: Alabama, Tennessee, South Carolina, North Carolina, Florida

How Georgia got its name: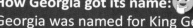
Georgia was named for King George II, who signed the charter for James Oglethorpe to found the colony.

Fun Laws:
• You cannot live on a boat for more than 30 days during the calendar year, even if just passing through the state.

Good to know!
• Atlanta, GA hosted the 1996 Centennial Summer Olympic Games.
• It is also called the Goober State because of all the peanuts they grow there.
• Martin Luther King Jr. was born in 1929 in Atlanta, Georgia.

23

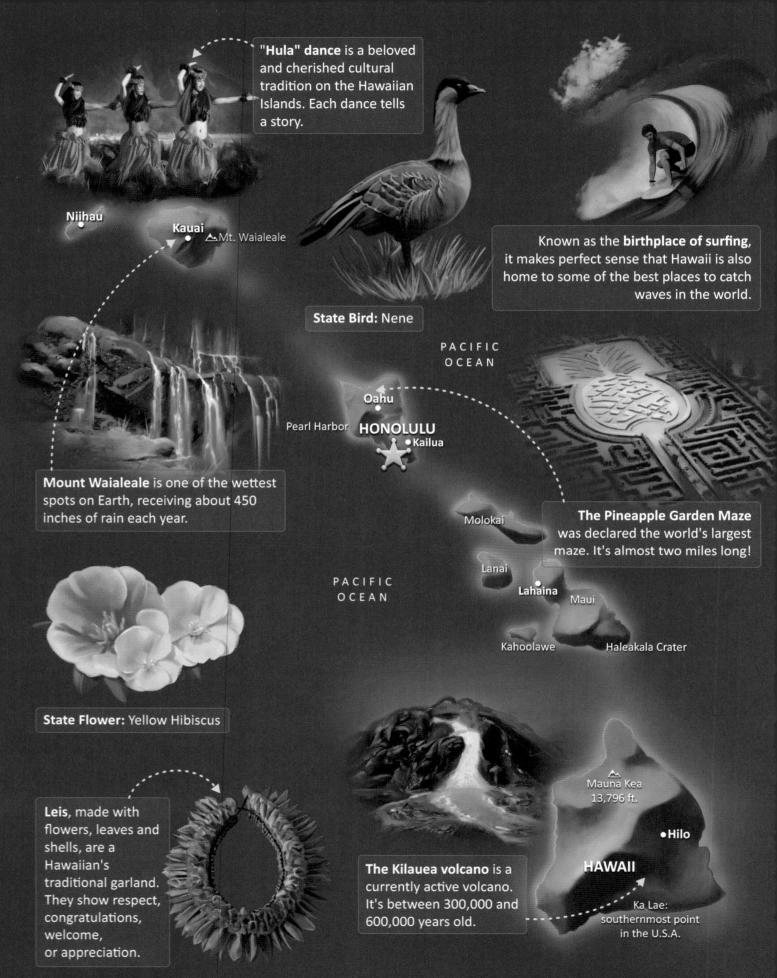

"Hula" dance is a beloved and cherished cultural tradition on the Hawaiian Islands. Each dance tells a story.

Known as the **birthplace of surfing**, it makes perfect sense that Hawaii is also home to some of the best places to catch waves in the world.

State Bird: Nene

Mount Waialeale is one of the wettest spots on Earth, receiving about 450 inches of rain each year.

The Pineapple Garden Maze was declared the world's largest maze. It's almost two miles long!

State Flower: Yellow Hibiscus

Leis, made with flowers, leaves and shells, are a Hawaiian's traditional garland. They show respect, congratulations, welcome, or appreciation.

The Kilauea volcano is a currently active volcano. It's between 300,000 and 600,000 years old.

PACIFIC OCEAN

PACIFIC OCEAN

Niihau

Kauai
⌂Mt. Waialeale

Oahu
Pearl Harbor
HONOLULU
•Kailua

Molokai

Lanai

Lahaina
Maui

Kahoolawe
Haleakala Crater

⌂ Mauna Kea 13,796 ft.

•Hilo

HAWAII

Ka Lae: southernmost point in the U.S.A.

24

HAWAII/HI

WELCOME TO THE ALOHA STATE

The Basics:
Total area: 10,932 sq. mi (28,313 sq. km)
Land area: 6,423 sq. mi (16,635 sq. km)
Population: 1,427,500
Capital: Honolulu

STORY TO KNOW

Hawaii, the last state, was 50th to be entered into the union, not until 1959. Their status as a state is still somewhat controversial, with many locals and native Hawaiian islanders resenting what they see as a forced colonization. These inhabitants are the descendants of a small handful of Polynesians who, some 1,500 years ago, travelled in canoes from the South Pacific to settle here. It wasn't until 1778, when Captain James Cook arrived and claimed the islands for Britain, that their way of life was ever interrupted. Cook would later be killed on these very islands, but they nonetheless became a center for whaling and sugarcane plantations.

Today, tourism and U.S. naval bases provide the primary economic institutions of the state, though agriculture in the form of sugarcane, pineapples, and other tropical crops are also a key industry. Famous for the "Aloha" spirit, the people and the culture of Hawaii are renowned for their kindness, generosity, and general friendliness. People from all over the world flock to these islands year-round to marvel at the lush tropical forests, soak in the sun along the white sandy beach shores, take a visit to the famed Pearl Harbor, and much, much more!

The State Motto: "THE LIFE OF THE LAND IS PERPETUATED IN RIGHTEOUSNESS"

The Facts: 🤓
Hawaii became the 50th state on August 21, 1959.
Major cities: Honolulu, Hilo, Kailua, Kaneohe, Waipahu
Border states: Does not border any other U.S. state

How Hawaii got its name: 😛
The name Hawaii comes from the name for the original home of the Polynesians, "Hawaiki."

Fun Laws: 😂
• In Hawaii, you will be fined for riding in the back of a passenger car without a seatbelt, however you can ride in the bed of a pickup truck with no safety equipment.

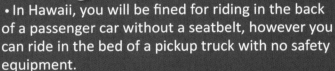

Good to know!
• Aloha" means love, affection, and mercy. It is used as a "hello" and "good-bye".
• This is the only state that grows coffee.
• There are 8 main islands that make up the state of Hawaii including. Maui, Niihau, Lanai, Kauai, Oahu, Molokai, Kahoolawe and the Island of Hawaii.
• The Hawaiian alphabet contains 12 letters: A, E, I, O, U, H, K, L, M, N, P, W.

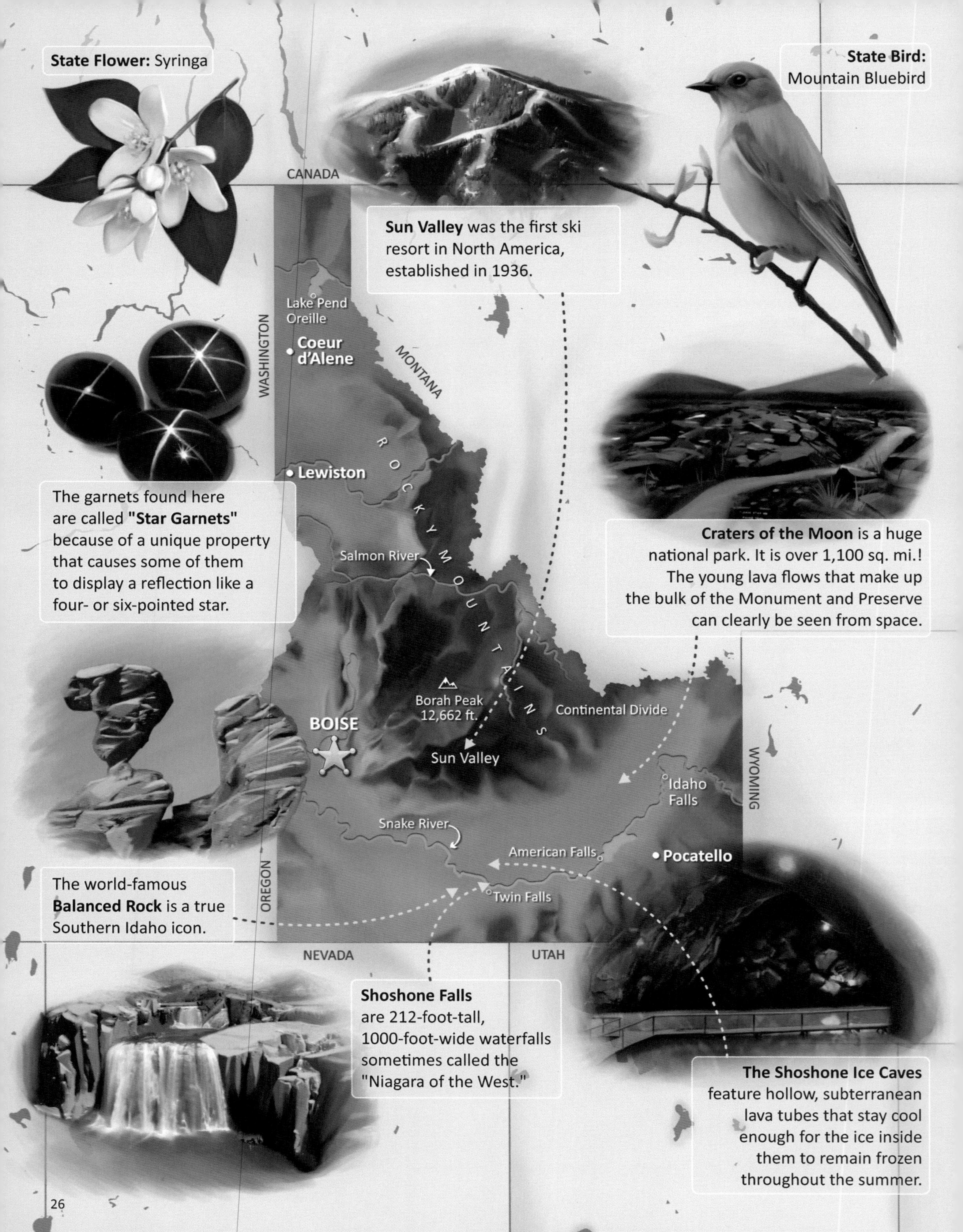

State Flower: Syringa

State Bird:
Mountain Bluebird

CANADA

Sun Valley was the first ski resort in North America, established in 1936.

Lake Pend Oreille

• **Coeur d'Alene**

WASHINGTON

MONTANA

The garnets found here are called **"Star Garnets"** because of a unique property that causes some of them to display a reflection like a four- or six-pointed star.

• **Lewiston**

R O C K Y   M O U N T A I N S

Salmon River

Craters of the Moon is a huge national park. It is over 1,100 sq. mi.! The young lava flows that make up the bulk of the Monument and Preserve can clearly be seen from space.

Borah Peak 12,662 ft.

Continental Divide

BOISE

Sun Valley

WYOMING

°Idaho Falls

Snake River

American Falls

• **Pocatello**

OREGON

The world-famous **Balanced Rock** is a true Southern Idaho icon.

°Twin Falls

NEVADA

UTAH

Shoshone Falls are 212-foot-tall, 1000-foot-wide waterfalls sometimes called the "Niagara of the West."

The Shoshone Ice Caves feature hollow, subterranean lava tubes that stay cool enough for the ice inside them to remain frozen throughout the summer.

IDAHO / ID

WELCOME TO THE GEM STATE

The Basics:
Total area: 83,569 sq. mi (216,443 sq. km)
Land area: 82,643 sq. mi (214,045 sq. km)
Population: 1,716,900
Capital: Boise

STORY TO KNOW

Idaho is one of the least densely populated states in the nation. Explored during the Lewis and Clark expeditions, many wagons eventually made their way across the state as part of the Oregon Trail. Contact throughout the state between Europeans and Native Americans brought disease and significant suffering to the indigenous people here, most of whom have been wiped out and no longer retain a presence. However, many of their artefacts and much of their cultural presence has been preserved, and some of the oldest anthropological finds in the country have been in Idaho, with obsidian arrowheads of the Shoshone and Nez Perce peoples.

The rugged forest and lake country of the north attracts tourists all year, and the farming country in the south makes up the majority of the state's economy. Potatoes are what it is perhaps best known for, but it's also a producer of dairy products, barley, wheat, and sugar beets. More modern industries such as manufacturing and technology have also begun to diversify this great state's economic picture.

The State Motto: "LET IT BE PERPETUAL"

The Facts: 😎
Idaho became the 43rd state on July 3, 1890.
Major cities: Boise, Idaho Falls, Nampa, Pocatello, Meridian
Border states: Utah, Wyoming, Montana, Washington, Oregon, Nevada

How Idaho got its name: 😋
Many people think that Idaho comes from a Native American word, but it does not. The name was actually just completely invented. It is often credited to Congressman George M. Willing.

Fun Laws: 😂 😂
• It's illegal for a man to give his sweetheart a box of candy weighing less than fifty pounds.

Good to know! 💡
• The Snake River travels all the way across Idaho.
• Idaho grows more potatoes than any other state.
• In 1995 Arco, Idaho became the first town in the world to be powered by atomic energy.

27

Cloud Gate (often locally called "The Bean") is a 110-ton elliptical sculpture forged of a seamless series of highly polished stainless-steel plates, which together reflect Chicago's famous skyline and the clouds above.

WISCONSIN

State Bird: Cardinal

The Ferris wheel may be one of the greatest inventions of all time. It turned 100 years old in 1993. The first Ferris wheel was built for the 1893 Chicago World's Fair.

• Rockford

Rock River

Chicago •

• Joliet

INDIANA

IOWA

Mississippi River

Illinois River

• Peoria

• Champaign

Sangamon River

SPRINGFIELD

Abraham Lincoln (1809 - 1865) began his political career in Illinois.

• Quincy

New • Salem

Decartur •

Kaskaskia River

Lake Shelbyville

Chicago is consistently named one of the best cities for St. Patrick's Day celebrations. The Chicago River is dyed green on this day.

○ Carlyle Lake

• East St. Louis

• Cahokia

Mississippi River

Wabash River

KENTUCKY

MISSOURI

Rend Lake

Big Muddy River

Ohio River

There are more nuclear power plants in Illinois than in any other state!

Starved Rock is one of Illinois' most beautiful destinations. In the winter, it freezes into spectacular icefalls!

State Flower: Violet

28

ILLINOIS/IL

WELCOME TO THE GARDEN OF THE WEST

The Basics:
Total area: 57,914 sq. mi (149,995 sq. km)
Land area: 55,519 sq. mi (143,793 sq. km)
Population: 12,802,000
Capital: Springfield

STORY TO KNOW

The French were the first to colonize Illinois in the late 1600s, and the Ohio river provided a steady stream of new settlers after that. By the 1830s, the Native Americans who had inhabited the area for thousands of years were pushed out. Illinois was the last state to join the union, and today it is a hub in the Midwest, with Chicago as the largest city in the region. This ethnically diverse city is situated right alongside Lake Michigan, and it serves as one of the largest air, highway, and rail centers in the country. The city has called numerous influential and important people residents: from the Obamas to Ronald Reagan, and from Abraham Lincoln to Hillary Clinton, some of America's most recognizable people hail from Illinois.

Apart from Chicago, the third-largest city in the US, the state is comprised of a rugged, forested southern region rife with coal deposits, the Great Leaks to the east and north, and fertile prairie soil in the central region. Chicago was host to the legendary 1893 World's Fair, a watershed moment in the industrial revolution which included the first Ferris Wheel and the first movie theater. Today, it has the Willis Tower, Wrigley Field, Millennium Park, the Old Navy Pier, and much more!

The State Motto: "STATE SOVEREIGNTY, NATIONAL UNION"

The Facts: 🤓
Illinois became the 21st state on December 3, 1818.
Major cities: Chicago, Aurora, Rockford, Joliet, Naperville, Springfield, Peoria
Border states: Missouri, Iowa, Wisconsin, Indiana, Kentucky

How Illinois got its name: 😜
The name Illinois is a French word that was used to describe the local Native Americans.

Fun Laws: 😂
• It is illegal to give a dog whiskey in Chicago.

Good to know! 💡
• Chicago is the third largest city in the United States.
• Famous people born in Illinois include Walt Disney, Harrison Ford, Ernest Hemingway, and President Ronald Reagan.
• Illinois was the first state to abolish slavery by ratifying the thirteenth amendment.

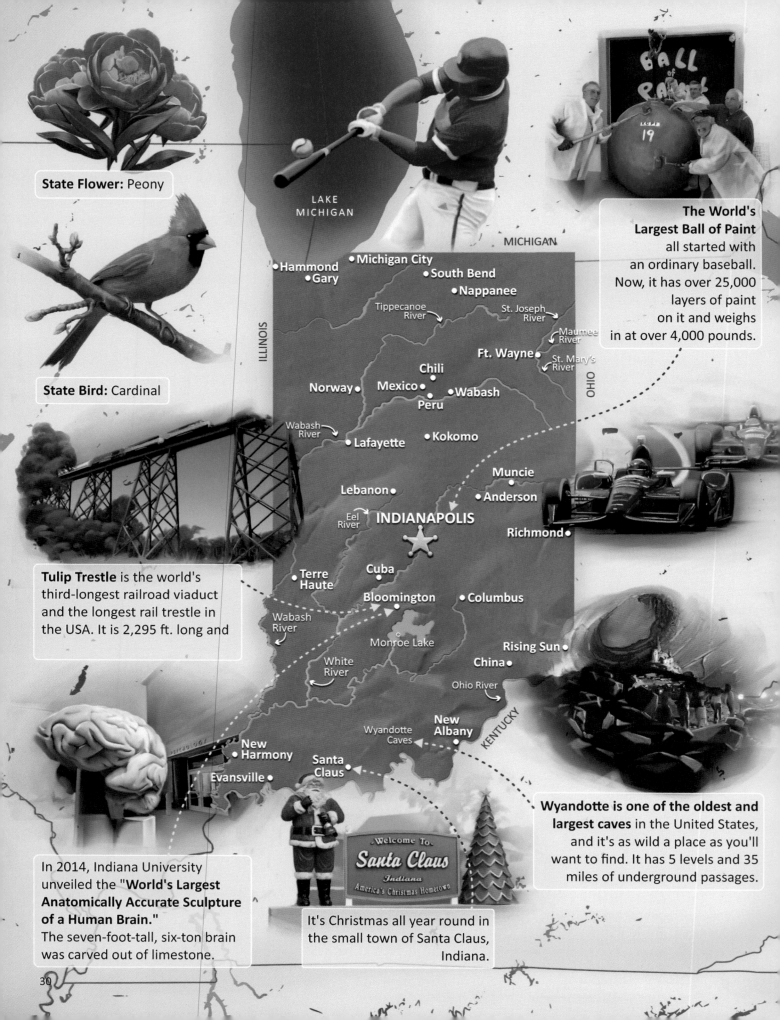

State Flower: Peony

State Bird: Cardinal

The World's Largest Ball of Paint all started with an ordinary baseball. Now, it has over 25,000 layers of paint on it and weighs in at over 4,000 pounds.

Tulip Trestle is the world's third-longest railroad viaduct and the longest rail trestle in the USA. It is 2,295 ft. long and

In 2014, Indiana University unveiled the "**World's Largest Anatomically Accurate Sculpture of a Human Brain.**" The seven-foot-tall, six-ton brain was carved out of limestone.

It's Christmas all year round in the small town of Santa Claus, Indiana.

Wyandotte is one of the oldest and largest caves in the United States, and it's as wild a place as you'll want to find. It has 5 levels and 35 miles of underground passages.

LAKE MICHIGAN

MICHIGAN

ILLINOIS

OHIO

KENTUCKY

Hammond
Michigan City
Gary
South Bend
Nappanee
Tippecanoe River
St. Joseph River
Maumee River
Ft. Wayne
St. Mary's River
Chili
Norway
Mexico
Wabash
Peru
Wabash River
Lafayette
Kokomo
Muncie
Lebanon
Anderson
Eel River
INDIANAPOLIS
Richmond
Cuba
Terre Haute
Bloomington
Columbus
Wabash River
Monroe Lake
Rising Sun
China
White River
Ohio River
New Albany
Wyandotte Caves
New Harmony
Santa Claus
Evansville

Welcome To Santa Claus Indiana America's Christmas Hometown

INDIANA /IN

WELCOME TO THE HOOSIER STATE

The Basics:
Total area: 36,420 sq. mi (94,326 sq. km)
Land area: 35,826 sq. mi (92,789 sq. km)
Population: 6,666,800
Capital: Indianapolis

STORY TO KNOW

Indiana, known first as the "Land of the Indians" and later as the "Crossroads of America," is situated dead center in the Midwest. Highways from all corners of the nation converge at its capital city of Indianapolis. The city is also famous for its Speedway, which hosts the Indy 500 every year in May. This race features a 500-mile high-octane endurance race often referred to as the "greatest spectacle in racing." Outside of the city, however, a more relaxing pace can be enjoyed: from lush forests to breezy cornfields and golden, lakeside sand dunes, Indiana is much more than just a motor city stopover.

Indiana joined the union later than most states in 1816, after which most of the last of its Native American inhabitants were forced out. Modern-day industries include tourism in the Great Lakes and Indianapolis, limestone quarries which have provided building material for the nation's buildings (including the Empire State Building!), auto racing, and agriculture/farming for corn, soybeans, and hogs. If you move here, you'll have a new title: residents of Indiana have been called Hoosiers for as long as the state's been around, though no one can quite seem to say why!

The State Motto: "THE CROSSROADS OF AMERICA"

The Facts: 😎
Indiana became the 19th state on December 11, 1816.
Major cities: Indianapolis, Fort Wayne, Evansville, South Bend, Carmel
Border states: Ohio, Kentucky, Illinois, Michigan

How Indiana got its name: 😊
The name Indiana refers to the local Native Americans and means "Land of the Indians."

Fun Laws: 😄
• Hotel sheets must be exactly 99 in. long and 81 in. wide.

Good to know! 💡
• The Indianapolis 500 Car Race is the biggest sporting event in the world. On May 31, 1911, the first race was held here.
• Indiana makes more popcorn than any other US state.
• The first professional baseball game was played in Fort Wayne, Indiana on May 4, 1871.

A 25-mile trail winds its way through five Iowa towns, from Woodward to Ankeny, with a dramatic crossing over the Des Moines River Valley. **The High Trestle Trail Bridge** is half a mile long and 130 ft. high, and is said to be among the largest trail bridges in the world.

Farmland is Iowa's most precious natural resource. Not only does it represent the basis for the state's agricultural production, but farmland represents over 100 billion dollars of wealth for Iowa.

The Mississippi River Valley is one of North America's greatest environmental resources and is a major bird migration corridor.

The National Balloon Classic is an annual event in Indianola that features hot air balloons, balloon rides, competitions, and family entertainment.

State Flower:
Wild Rose

State Bird: Goldfinch

The US is the world leader in corn production, after growing 15.1 billion bushels in 2017. No state grows more corn than Iowa, which produced 2.7 billion of those bushels.

Grant Wood's painting **American Gothic** brought an 1880s Iowan farmhouse into the public eye as the backdrop of a now-famous image of a Midwestern farmer and his daughter. Hundreds of parodies and homages have today made it a popular cultural icon that is one of the most recognized paintings in the world.

MINNESOTA

SOUTH DAKOTA

Big Sioux River

Spirit Lake

Little Sioux River

Cedar River

Turkey River

Hawkeye

WISCONSIN

Sioux City

Storm Lake

Ft. Dodge

Cedar Falls

Waterloo

Raccoon River

Iowa River

Wapsipinicon River

Ames

Cedar Rapids

Amana

Clinton

DES MOINES

Iowa City

Davenport

NEBRASKA

East Peru

Skunk River

Council Bluffs

Des Moines River

Rathbun Reservoir

MISSOURI

Burlington

ILLINOIS

Keokuk

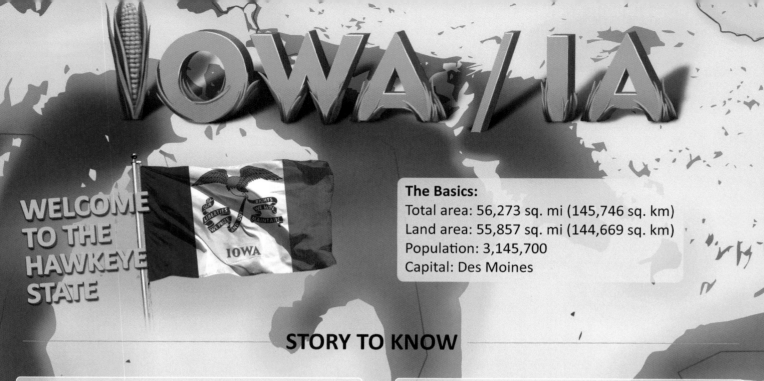

IOWA/IA

WELCOME TO THE HAWKEYE STATE

The Basics:
Total area: 56,273 sq. mi (145,746 sq. km)
Land area: 55,857 sq. mi (144,669 sq. km)
Population: 3,145,700
Capital: Des Moines

STORY TO KNOW

Iowa may not be the most well-known state, but it's not lacking in excitement, beauty, or productivity. Every year in August sees the Iowa State Fair, one of the largest in the country, and hundreds of thousands of visitors pass through. On display is Iowa's agriculture, of which its residents are fiercely proud, its cuisine, and a great deal more – including a 600-pound butter sculpture of a cow! This rich agricultural sector provides over a tenth of all of America's food, and much of its livestock is destined for dinner plates across the country and around the world.

Iowa became the 29th state in 1836, with settlers from Germany, Scandinavia, Slovakia, and many other places all calling the region home. The earliest dwellers were the Sauk Indians, whose chief, Black Hawk, gives the state its name: The Hawkeye State. Their prehistoric ancestors left behind earthen mounds in the shapes of bears and birds in Northeastern Iowa, and this area still draws tourists to this day. As for modern-day Iowa, with its ample precipitation and rich soil, it continues to be the country's top producer of corn, soybeans, eggs, and hogs.

The State Motto: "OUR LIBERTIES WE PRIZE AND OUR RIGHTS WE WILL MAINTAIN"

The Facts: 😎
Iowa became the 29th state on December 28, 1846.
Major cities: Des Moines, Cedar Rapids, Davenport, Sioux City, Waterloo
Border states: Wisconsin, Illinois, Missouri, Nebraska, South Dakota, Minnesota

How Iowa got its name: 😛
The name comes from the Ioway, one of the Native American tribes that lived in the region.

Fun Laws: 😂 😂
• A man with a moustache may never kiss a woman in public.
• Kisses may last for no more than five minutes.

Good to know! 💥
• Iowa played a key role in the Underground Railroad that rescued slaves from the South.
• The eastern and western borders of Iowa are entirely made of water. The Mississippi River forms the border to the east and the Missouri River to the west.
• In 1907 Fred Maytag invented the clothes washing machine in Newton, Iowa.

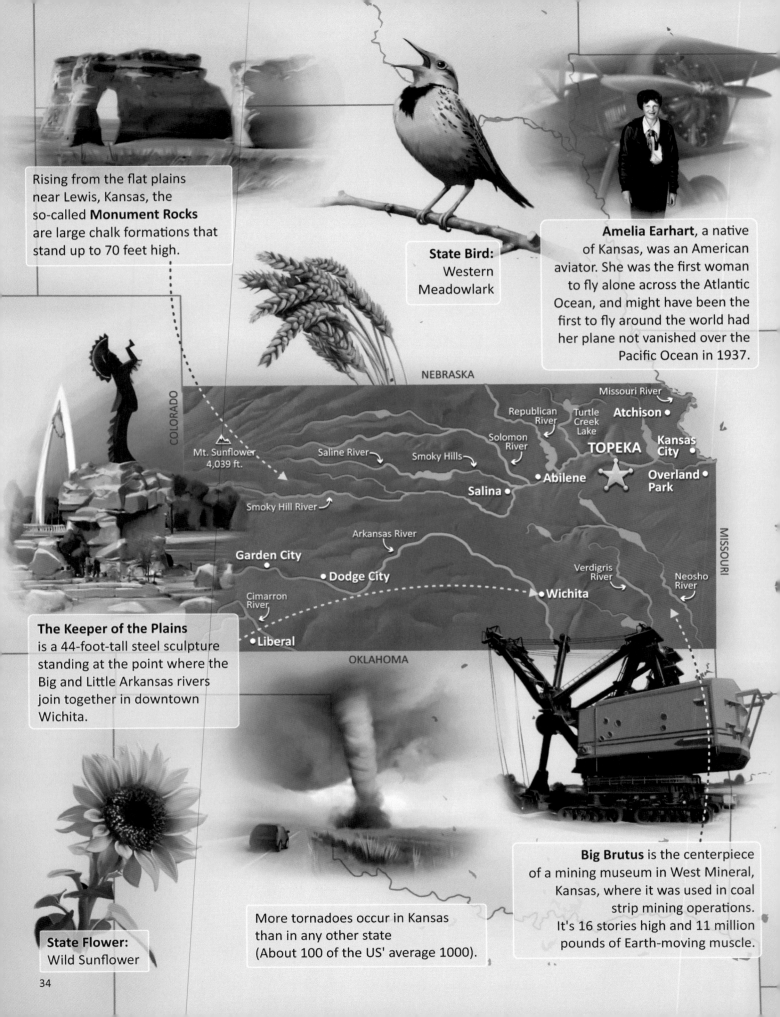

Rising from the flat plains near Lewis, Kansas, the so-called **Monument Rocks** are large chalk formations that stand up to 70 feet high.

State Bird: Western Meadowlark

Amelia Earhart, a native of Kansas, was an American aviator. She was the first woman to fly alone across the Atlantic Ocean, and might have been the first to fly around the world had her plane not vanished over the Pacific Ocean in 1937.

NEBRASKA

Missouri River

Republican River   Turtle Creek Lake   **Atchison**

Solomon River

TOPEKA   **Kansas City**

Mt. Sunflower 4,039 ft.   Saline River   Smoky Hills   **Abilene**   **Overland Park**

COLORADO

Salina

Smoky Hill River

Arkansas River

MISSOURI

Garden City

Verdigris River   Neosho River

Dodge City

Cimarron River   **Wichita**

Liberal

OKLAHOMA

The Keeper of the Plains is a 44-foot-tall steel sculpture standing at the point where the Big and Little Arkansas rivers join together in downtown Wichita.

Big Brutus is the centerpiece of a mining museum in West Mineral, Kansas, where it was used in coal strip mining operations. It's 16 stories high and 11 million pounds of Earth-moving muscle.

More tornadoes occur in Kansas than in any other state (About 100 of the US' average 1000).

State Flower: Wild Sunflower

KANSAS/KS

WELCOME TO THE SUNFLOWER STATE

The Basics:
Total area: 82,278 sq. mi (213,100 sq. km)
Land area: 81,759 sq. mi (211,754 sq. km)
Population: 2,913,100
Capital: Topeka

STORY TO KNOW

The original tracts of land comprising modern-day Kansas were considered uninhabitable by early settlers, and they were handed over as Indian territory in the 1830s. By the time the Civil War was nearly upon the nation, however, colonizers were fighting for more land and inevitably they pushed into the Indian territory they had granted just decades earlier. This became the early frontier of the wild west, with Texas cattle ranchers and railroaders from the east moving into the Kansas plains. As the state moves west, it eventually breaks ground to the majestic Rocky Mountains!

Today, the wide prairies of Kansas are home to some of the most cattle per capita in the country. Its occasionally extreme weather in the form of thunderstorms and tornadoes aside, Kansas is known for its sunshine and tranquil beauty. Oil and gas throughout the state, and aircraft manufacturing in Wichita, its largest city, are the main industries here. Full of history, from museums to Civil War battlefields, and made famous as Dorothy's home in the Wizard of Oz, there truly is no place like home in Kansas!

The State Motto: "TO THE STARS THROUGH DIFFICULTIES"

The Facts: 😎
Kansas became the 34th state on January 29, 1861.
Major cities: Wichita, Overland Park, Kansas City, Topeka, Olathe, Lawrence
Border states: Missouri, Nebraska, Colorado, Oklahoma

How Kansas got its name:
The name Kansas comes from a local Native American tribe called the Kansa (also Kaw). The name means "People of the south wind."

Fun Laws: 😄 😄
• No one may catch fish with his bare hands.

Good to know! 💡
• Kansas has so many tornadoes, it has the nickname "Tornado Alley".
• Smith County is the center of the 48 contiguous United States.
• Kansas produces enough wheat in a year to provide every person on earth with six loaves of bread.

State Bird:
Kentucky Cardinal

Fort Knox is perhaps best-known as the United States Bullion Depository, or "Gold Vault" as it is affectionately called by millions around the world. The facility, with its security systems shrouded in secrecy, houses the largest portion of the United States' gold reserve.

The Kentucky Vietnam Veterans Memorial overlooks the state Capitol and honors the 125,000 Kentuckians who served this nation so courageously and unselfishly during the Vietnam war era (1962-1975).

Kentucky is one of the birthplaces of bluegrass music. The father of this genre was Bill Monroe.

Covington

Ohio River

OHIO

FRANKFORT

Ashland

Big Sandy River

INDIANA

Louisville

Salt River

Lexington

Tug Fork River

Owensboro Fort Knox

Rough River

Hodgeville

Kentucky River

Green River

Mammoth Cave

Cumberland River

APPALACHIAN MOUNTAINS

ILLINOIS

Lake Barkley

Black Mountain 4,145 ft.

MISSOURI

Paducah

Mississippi River

Kentucky Lake

Lake Cumberland

Cumberland Gap

VIRGINIA

TENNESSEE

State Flower:
Goldenrod

Mammoth Cave is one of the world's longest known caves - more than 365 miles have been explored so far. Over 200 animal species are found there.

Abraham Lincoln, the 16th president of the USA, was born in **Hodgenville, Kentucky.**

Known as the "Niagara of the South," **Cumberland Falls** is the largest waterfall south of the Niagara. A 125 ft. wide wall of water drops into a boulder-strewn gorge.

KENTUCKY/KY

WELCOME TO THE BLUEGRASS STATE

The Basics:
Total area: 40,408 sq. mi (104,656 sq. km)
Land area: 39,486 sq. mi (102,269 sq. km)
Population: 4,454,200
Capital: Frankfort

STORY TO KNOW

The first settlers in Kentucky staked their claim in 1775, just before the Revolutionary War, after signing treaties with the resident Cherokee peoples. This central state was the 15th to join the union, and ever since it has held much of what America has to offer within it – mining and industry in the north, the charm and comfort of the south, tradition in the east, and a wild west of its own. Although the mining industry has done considerable damage to Kentucky's magnificent landscapes, modern regulations aim to reverse this and restore the state's natural beauty.

Kentucky is home to sections of the Appalachia, and it's famous both for its whiskey and for the Kentucky Derby, held each year in Louisville. With some of the most expansive horse country in the nation, the world's top racehorses are bred here, providing economic stability to ranchers, breeders, and those in the racing industry alike. Fans of other outdoor activities will not be bored here either, with kayaking, mountaineering, river rafting, camping, fishing, and caving all on offer. This beautiful state has the greatest number of miles of running water in the entire continental US!

The State Motto: "UNITED WE STAND, DIVIDED WE FALL"

The Facts: 😎
Kentucky became the 15th state on June 1, 1792.
Major cities: Louisville, Lexington, Bowling Green, Owensboro, Covington
Border states: Ohio, Indiana, Illinois, Missouri, Tennessee, West Virginia, Virginia

How Kentucky got its name: 😜
The name for Kentucky comes from a Native American Iroquois word "Ken-tah-ten," meaning "Land of tomorrow."

Fun Laws: 😁
• One may not dye a duckling blue and offer it for sale unless more than six are for sale at once.
• Dogs may not molest cars in Fort Thomas, Kentucky.

Good to know! 💡
• The Kentucky Derby is one of the world's most famous horse races.
• Kentucky is one of three states, including Colorado and California, who claim to have invented the cheeseburger.
• The song 'Happy Birthday to You' was written by two sisters in Louisville.

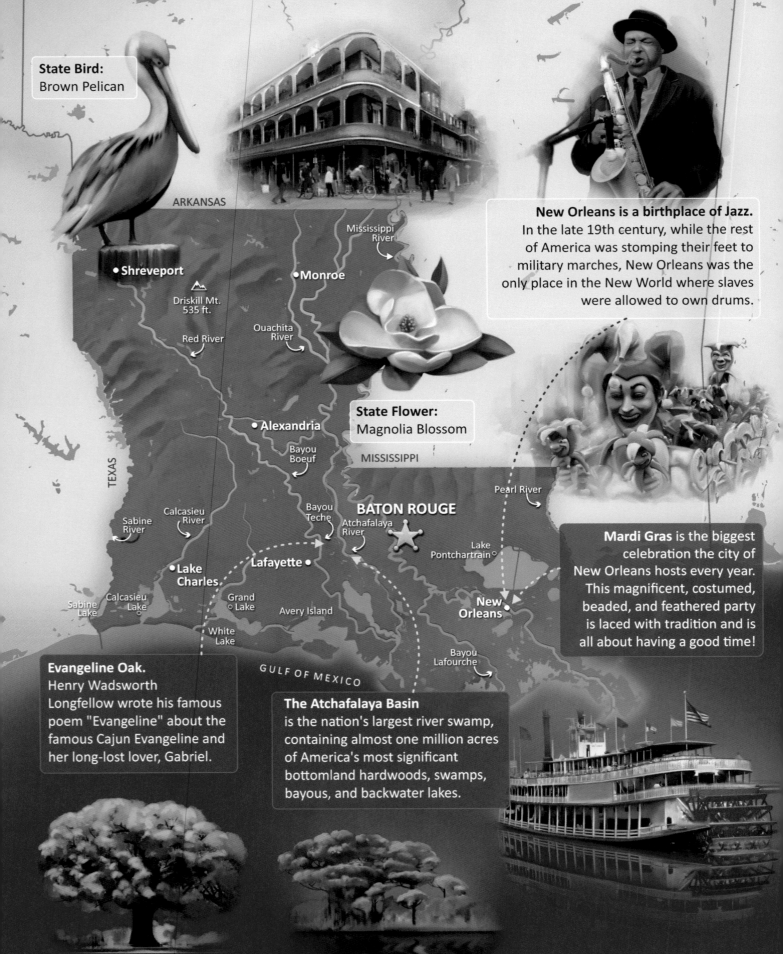

State Bird:
Brown Pelican

ARKANSAS

Mississippi River

New Orleans is a birthplace of Jazz.
In the late 19th century, while the rest of America was stomping their feet to military marches, New Orleans was the only place in the New World where slaves were allowed to own drums.

• Shreveport

• Monroe

Driskill Mt. 535 ft.

Red River

Ouachita River

State Flower:
Magnolia Blossom

MISSISSIPPI

• Alexandria

Bayou Boeuf

TEXAS

Calcasieu River

Bayou Teche

Pearl River

Atchafalaya River

BATON ROUGE

Lake Pontchartrain

Sabine River

Lafayette •

Mardi Gras is the biggest celebration the city of New Orleans hosts every year. This magnificent, costumed, beaded, and feathered party is laced with tradition and is all about having a good time!

• Lake Charles

Sabine Lake

Calcasieu Lake

Grand Lake

Avery Island

New Orleans

White Lake

Bayou Lafourche

GULF OF MEXICO

Evangeline Oak.
Henry Wadsworth Longfellow wrote his famous poem "Evangeline" about the famous Cajun Evangeline and her long-lost lover, Gabriel.

The Atchafalaya Basin
is the nation's largest river swamp, containing almost one million acres of America's most significant bottomland hardwoods, swamps, bayous, and backwater lakes.

LOUISIANA/LA

WELCOME TO THE PELICAN STATE

The Basics:
Total area: 52,378 sq. mi (135,659 sq. km)
Land area: 43,204 sq. mi (111,898 sq. km)
Population: 4,684,300
Capital: Baton Rouge

STORY TO KNOW

The historic Louisiana Purchase was made in 1803 when the United States bought an enormous section of land from France. Today, this region spans 15 states, and modern Louisiana isn't quite so large. It hasn't lost any of its charm or intrigue, however! From festivals like the Mardi Gras in New Orleans to delicious cuisine you won't find anywhere else on Earth, this state boasts a wealth of southern charm and a colorful history.

Louisiana has also had its fair share of adversity – Hurricane Katrina and the Deepwater Horizon oil rig explosion both hit the state hard. Through their recovery efforts, residents of Louisiana showed the world their strength, courage, and resolve. Today, the scars of these and other disasters can still be seen, but the people and their culture still shine as brightly as ever. Its ports still carry imports and exports to and from the United States and around the world, and oil and gas continues to support the economy. The Creole cuisine and the delicious seafood still warm the streets with their scrumptious aromas. One thing is for sure: Louisiana isn't going anywhere!

The State Motto: "UNION, JUSTICE, AND CONFIDENCE"

The Facts: 🤓
Louisiana became the 18th state on April 30, 1812.
Major cities: New Orleans, Baton Rouge, Shreveport, Metairie, Lafayette
Border states: Mississippi, Arkansas, Texas

How Louisiana got its name: 😛
Louisiana was named after Louis XIV, the King of France.

Fun Laws: 😄
• Persons could land in jail for up to ten years for stealing an alligator.
• It is a $500 fine to instruct a pizza delivery man to deliver a pizza to your friend without them knowing.

Good to know! 💡
• New Orleans is known as the Jazz Capital of the world.
• Louisiana was part of the Louisiana Territory that the US bought from France in 1803 for $15 million.

State Bird:
Chickadee

The official state cat of Maine is - you guessed it - **the Maine Coon**. This plus-sized cat is likely the oldest cat breed native to America.

Moosehead Lake, in the heart of the Maine Highlands region, is the state's largest body of water. This place is home to many moose.

Eartha, housed in a three-story glass gallery at DeLorme Headquarters, is the world's largest spinning globe.

CANADA

St. John River

Allagash River

Aroostook River

CANADA

Moosehead Lake

Mt. Katahdin 5,268 ft.

WHITE MOUNTAINS

Piscataquis River

Grando Lake

Penobscot River

Bangor •

Machias River

Androscoggin River

Kennebec River

AUGUSTA

NEW HAMPSHIRE

Sebago Lake

Portland •

State Flower:
White Pine

ATLANTIC OCEAN

Kennebunkport •

Maine lobsters are world-famous and sold annually

Portland Head Light, built during the presidency of George Washington, is one of Maine's iconic lighthouses.

Maine's Atlantic coast is very rocky.

MAINE/ME

WELCOME TO THE PINE TREE STATE

The Basics:
Total area: 35,380 sq. mi (91,633 sq. km)
Land area: 30,843 sq. mi (79,883 sq. km)
Population: 1,335,900
Capital: Augusta

STORY TO KNOW

Maine serves as a reminder that big things often come in small packages. It has long been home to some of America's earliest settlers, and in fact was inhabited by indigenous peoples for thousands of years prior to colonization. It was likely even visited by Leif Erikson and his Viking voyage as many as 500 years before modern Europeans ever set foot there! In the modern day, it remains one of few states that retains some of its old-world charm. A robust fishing and timber industry, combined with ample tourism, give it a healthy economy, and the rugged beauty of its coastline is an inspiration to its residents and visitors alike.

Maine has provided numerous authors and novelists with material for their greatest works. Stephen King is perhaps most famous among them, though Robert McCloskey and E. B. White (*Charlotte's Web*) are in the running as well. From writing to oil paintings to folklore and legend, Maine is steeped in history, mystery, and beauty. Its inhabitants asserted their independence in 1820 through the Missouri Compromise, and they have remained a proud and hearty people ever since.

The State Motto: "I LEAD"

The Facts:
Maine became the 23rd state on March 15, 1820.
Major cities: Portland, Lewiston, Bangor, Auburn, Biddeford
Border states: New Hampshire

How Maine got its name:
There is no clear answer as to where the name Maine came from. It first appeared in a charter that granted land to Sir Ferdinando Gorges and Captain John Mason. When the land was split between the two, the land that was Gorges' became known as Maine. It is likely that the name came from a nautical reference to the mainland.

Fun Laws:
• You may not step out of a plane in flight.

Good to know!
• Writers Stephen King and Henry Wadsworth Longfellow were both born in Maine.
• Maine has over 2,000 islands and 6,000 lakes and ponds.
• When people say 'bugs' in Maine they are often referring to lobsters.

State Bird:
Baltimore Oriole

The Wye Oak tree is the largest white oak in the United States. Estimated to be more than 400 years old, it stands 107 ft. tall and measures 34½ feet around at its base.

Maryland designated **calico** as its official state cat in 2001. Calico is not a breed of cat, but an unusual coloring (orange, black, and white) that occurs across many breeds.

PENNSYLVANIA

WEST VIRGINIA

ALLEGHENY MOUNTAINS

VIRGINIA

Patuxent River

Potomac River

Baltimore

ANNAPOLIS

Bethesda

WASHINGTON, D.C.

Wye Mills

DELAWARE

Cambridge

Potomac River

Assateague Island

The National Aquarium, which opened in 1981 in Baltimore, is one of the largest public aquariums in the United States. Of the more than 10,000 marine and freshwater animals maintained by the aquarium, many are marine mammals, birds, reptiles, and amphibians.

State Flower:
Black-eyed Susan

Chesapeake Bay

Assateague wild ponies have roamed the beaches, pine forests, and salt marshes of Assateague Island since the 1600s. **Assateague Island National Seashore** has a combined total of over 300 wild ponies between Maryland and Virginia.

MARYLAND / MD

WELCOME TO THE MONUMENTAL STATE

The Basics:
Total area: 12,406 sq. mi (32,131 sq. km)
Land area: 9,707 sq. mi (25,142 sq. km)
Population: 6,052,200
Capital: Annapolis

STORY TO KNOW

Maryland is often called "America in Miniature," and for good reason! It is home to pine groves, mountains, sandy beaches, quiet fishing villages, and bustling cities. As the seventh state, it also has considerable historical significance: it houses the longest continuously-used capital building, and a small cadre 400 strong of Maryland soldiers held back an enormous British force in the Revolutionary War, allowing George Washington and his men to escape. This earned it the nickname "Old Line State."

Perhaps Maryland's most famous geographical feature is Chesapeake Bay, where the state's original inhabitants grew crops and harvested oysters for thousands of years before colonization in the early 1600s. This bay is the largest estuary in the continental United States, splitting Maryland into two distinct regions: a mountainous panhandle in the West and a flat coastal plain in the East. Today, Maryland is a hub for government, research, and high-tech business, providing an urban corridor to the nation's capital in Washington D.C.

The State Motto: "STRONG DEEDS, GENTLE WORDS"

The Facts: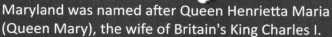
Maryland became the 7th state on April 28, 1788.
Major cities: Baltimore, Columbia, Germantown, Silver Spring, Waldorf
Border states: Pennsylvania, Delaware, Virginia, West Virginia, Washington D.C

How Maryland got its name:
Maryland was named after Queen Henrietta Maria (Queen Mary), the wife of Britain's King Charles I.

Fun Laws:
• Thistles may not grow in one's yard.
• It's illegal to take a lion to the movies in Baltimore, Maryland.

Good to know!
• The refrigerator was invented in Baltimore by Thomas Moore in 1803.
• The first successful manned balloon launch in the US was in Baltimore. The rider was a 13-year-old boy named Edward Warren.

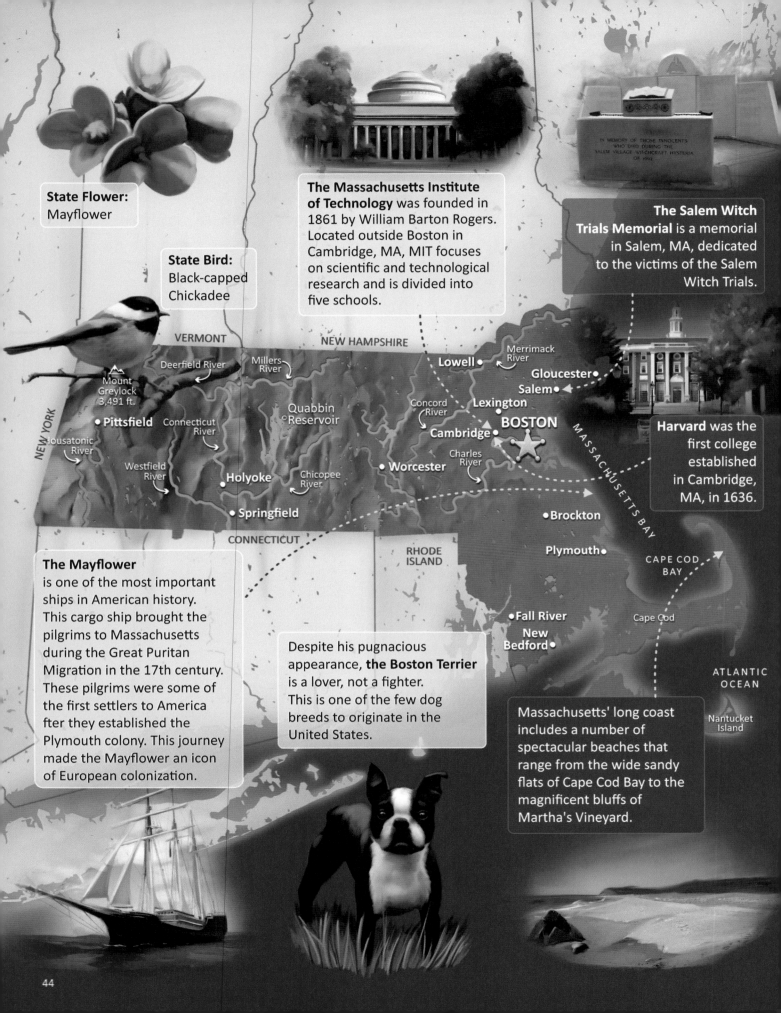

State Flower:
Mayflower

State Bird:
Black-capped Chickadee

The Massachusetts Institute of Technology was founded in 1861 by William Barton Rogers. Located outside Boston in Cambridge, MA, MIT focuses on scientific and technological research and is divided into five schools.

The Salem Witch Trials Memorial is a memorial in Salem, MA, dedicated to the victims of the Salem Witch Trials.

Harvard was the first college established in Cambridge, MA, in 1636.

The Mayflower is one of the most important ships in American history. This cargo ship brought the pilgrims to Massachusetts during the Great Puritan Migration in the 17th century. These pilgrims were some of the first settlers to America fter they established the Plymouth colony. This journey made the Mayflower an icon of European colonization.

Despite his pugnacious appearance, **the Boston Terrier** is a lover, not a fighter. This is one of the few dog breeds to originate in the United States.

Massachusetts' long coast includes a number of spectacular beaches that range from the wide sandy flats of Cape Cod Bay to the magnificent bluffs of Martha's Vineyard.

VERMONT

NEW HAMPSHIRE

NEW YORK

Mount Greylock 3,491 ft.

Deerfield River

Millers River

Connecticut River

Housatonic River

Pittsfield

Westfield River

Holyoke

Quabbin Reservoir

Chicopee River

Springfield

CONNECTICUT

RHODE ISLAND

Lowell

Merrimack River

Concord River

Gloucester

Salem

Lexington

Cambridge

BOSTON

Worcester

Charles River

MASSACHUSETTS BAY

Brockton

Plymouth

CAPE COD BAY

Cape Cod

Fall River

New Bedford

ATLANTIC OCEAN

Nantucket Island

MASSACHUSETTS/MA

WELCOME TO THE BAY STATE

The Basics:
Total area: 10,554 sq. mi (27,336 sq. km)
Land area: 7,800 sq. mi (20,202 sq. km)
Population: 6,859,800
Capital: Boston

STORY TO KNOW

Massachusetts, the Bay State, is home to pioneers of all stripes. Inhabited for thousands of years by Native Americans, visited by Norse explorers a thousand years ago, and one of the first states to join the modern Union, Massachusetts represents nearly everything America stands for: industry, creativity, innovation, diversity, and freedom. The early colonial settlers were almost all of them fleeing religious persecution in Europe, and as such, their region (modern day Massachusetts) represents a strong current of religious freedom.

With 114 colleges and universities across the state, it's no stretch to say that Massachusetts is host to renowned academic talent. World-class inventors, scientists, researchers, and artists have all called the state their home, from literary giant Emily Dickinson in Amherst to the Ivy League halls of Harvard. The Bay State's historical and modern-day thriving steel and iron industries keep it from ascending too high into the lofty ivory tower and help make Massachusetts an economic powerhouse considering its size. With all of this hustle and bustle, it still manages to present rugged natural beauty, particularly in the summer time, when its white sand, cool water, cheese and wine counties, and seafood are all ripe for enjoyment.

The State Motto: "BY THE SWORD WE SEEK PEACE, BUT PEACE ONLY UNDER LIBERTY"

The Facts:
Massachusetts became the 6th state on February 6, 1788.
Major cities: Boston, Worcester, Springfield, Lowell, Cambridge, New Bedford
Border states: Rhode Island, Connecticut, New York, Vermont, New Hampshire

How Massachusetts got its name:
The name comes from the Native American Algonquian language. It means "Big hill place."

Fun Laws:
• Quakers and witches are banned.
• No gorilla is allowed in the back seat of any car.

Good to know!
• The first baseball World Series was held in Boston in 1903.
• Four US presidents were born in Massachusetts. They include John Adams, John Quincy Adams, John Fitzgerald Kennedy and George H. W. Bush.

State Bird: Robin

Isle Royale is one of the most beautiful and wondrous places in the United States. It's a home to moose and wolves.

The Mackinac Bridge is the longest suspension bridge in the Western Hemisphere, with 7,400 ft. of roadway suspended in the air over the straits of Mackinac.

Copper Harbor •

KEWEENAW BAY

PORCUPINE MOUNTAINS

Mt. Curwood 1,980 ft.

LAKE SUPERIOR

• Ironwood

Escanaba River

Manistique River

Sault • Sainte Marie

CANADA

WISCONSIN

Escanaba •

GREEN BAY

○ Mackinac Island

State Flower: Apple Blossom

LAKE MICHIGAN

Traverse City

Au Sable River

LAKE HURON

An 8,000-pound, 24 ft. bronze arm and fist was sculpted in Michigan to honor the great boxer Joe Louis.

Manistee River

○ Houghton Lake

SAGINAW BAY

Muskegon River

Bay City •

• Saginaw

• Muskegon

Grand River

Saginaw River

Port Huron

LANSING

• Flint

Frozen Pier. During winter, the waves crash up onto this pier and freeze to it. As a result, amazing ice formations cover the lighthouses and look like something from a fairy tale.

Grand Rapids

Kalamazoo River

Pontiac

St. Clair River

Detroit • LAKE ST. CLAIR

Dearborn •

Kalamazoo •

• Battle Creek

LAKE ERIE

INDIANA

OHIO

Ann Arbor •

ILLINOIS

The Cereal Bowl of America. Battle Creek, where the leading producers of ready-to-eat cereals are located, produces more breakfast cereals than anywhere in the world!

Henry Ford invented his first vehicle on June 4, 1896. It was powered by a four-horsepower engine. Instead of a steering wheel, the Quadricycle had a tiller. The gearbox had only two forward gears with no reverse.

MICHIGAN/MI

WELCOME TO THE GREAT LAKES STATE

The Basics:
Total area: 96,714 sq. mi (250,487 sq. km)
Land area: 56,539 sq. mi (146,435 sq. km)
Population: 9,962,300
Capital: Lansing

STORY TO KNOW

The northerly state of Michigan rests against four of the five Great Lakes, giving it the obvious title of the "Great Lakes State." The lower peninsula is called home to most of the state's residents, and the upper peninsula sees vacationers and adventurers year-round. The state is perhaps most famous in the modern-day for its auto industry, with the rise and fall of the "Big Three" catapulting Michigan through prosperity and down into poverty as manufacturing jobs were automated and moved elsewhere. Nowhere is this more evident, perhaps, than in its most famous cities, Flint and Detroit.

Detroit is home to Motown, the historic record label, and was the place where the Ford Model T was first mass produced. It's also a gateway to Canada, and Michigan sees billions of dollars of trade with that country passing through each year. Beyond cities and the auto industry, the state also has a robust agriculture sector, growing everything from grains to fruits, and tourism is also on the rise. There is natural wonder and cultural history from the Native Americans to be found in the 26th state, and it may just be worth staying a while!

The State Motto: "IF YOU SEEK A PLEASANT PENINSULA, LOOK AROUND YOU"

The Facts: 🤓
Michigan became the 26th state on January 26, 1837.
Major cities: Detroit, Grand Rapids, Warren, Sterling Heights, Ann Arbor, Lansing
Border states: Ohio, Indiana, Wisconsin, Minnesota (via Lake Superior)

How Michigan got its name: 🤪
The name Michigan comes from an Algonquian Indian word that means "Big water."

Fun Laws: 😆 😆
• Cars may not be sold on Sunday.
• A woman isn't allowed to cut her own hair without her husband's permission.

Good to know!
• Michigan borders four of the five Great Lakes (Lake Superior, Lake Michigan, Lake Huron, and Lake Erie).
• Detroit is the car capital of the world with General Motors, Chrysler, and Ford. It is often called Motor Town or Motown.
• No matter where you are in Michigan, you are always within 85 miles of a Great Lake.

State Bird: Common Loon

Boundary Waters Canoe Area.
This area contains more than 1,200 miles of canoe routes, 12 hiking trails, and over 2,000 designated campsites. No cars or hotels are allowed in this area.

The International Wolf Center advances the survival of wolf populations by teaching about wolves, their relationship to wildlands, and the human role in their future.

Lake Mille Lacs. There's something about sitting in a toasty warm ice house, just waiting for that lunker to nibble on your hook. You can find a lot of fishing houses here during the winter time.

Red River
Lake of the woods
Rainy River
International Falls
CANADA
BOUDARY WATERS CANOE AREA
Upper Red Lake
Lower Red Lake
Lake Winnibigoshish
Ely
Eagle Mt. 2,301 ft.
St. Louis River
Grand Rapids
Duluth
Leech Lake
Crow Wing River
Mille Lacs Lake
NORTH DAKOTA
Mississippi River
St. Croix River
Big Stone Lake
St. Cloud
WISCONSIN
SOUTH DAKOTA
Minnesota River
Lake Minnetonka
St. PAUL
Minneapolis
Lake Pepin
Pipestone
Mankato
Mississippi River
IOWA

Lake Superior is the world's largest freshwater lake. Its surface area (31,700 sq. mi or 82,170 sq. km) is greater than the combined areas of Vermont, Massachusetts, Rhode Island, Connecticut, and New Hampshire.

State Flower: Pink and White Lady's Slipper

Focusing on the visual, performing, and media arts of our time, **the Walker Art Center** takes a global, multidisciplinary, and diverse approach to the creation, presentation, interpretation, collection, and preservation of art.

Built in 1910, **the Fitzgerald Theater** is Saint Paul's oldest surviving theater. All of its 1000 seats are no further than 87 ft. from the stage.

MINNESOTA / MN

WELCOME TO THE LAND OF LAKES

The Basics:
Total area: 86,936 sq. mi (225,163 sq. km)
Land area: 79,627 sq. mi (206,232 sq. km)
Population: 5,576,600
Capital: Saint Paul

STORY TO KNOW

Minnesota, often called "The Land of 10,000 Lakes," actually contains a far greater number even than that! Raw, wild nature and an abundance of natural resources have been the mainstays of Minnesota for centuries, well before it became a state in 1858. The land is rich in wildlife, forest, timber, fertile soil, fresh water, and minerals. This has led to large industries in agriculture, forestry, and mining. Minnesota produces more iron ore than any other state in America! Most of this ore is shipped through the city of Duluth.

Minnesota's twin cities of St. Paul and Minneapolis represent the source headwaters of the great Mississippi, flowing down from Lake Itasca. These cities are home to residents of all kinds, be they industry workers, students, vacationers, government workers, artists (F. Scott Fitzgerald and Bob Dylan both grew up here!), and many others. Adventurers and outdoorspeople from across the country and around the world have Minnesota as a prime destination for their activities. From hiking to mountain biking to skiing and camping, there is something for nearly everyone here, any time of year.

The State Motto: "THE STAR OF THE NORTH"

The Facts: 😎
Minnesota became the 32nd state on May 11, 1858.
Major cities: Minneapolis, Saint Paul, Rochester, Duluth, Bloomington
Border states: North Dakota, South Dakota, Iowa, Wisconsin, Michigan (at Lake Superior)

How Minnesota got its name:
The name Minnesota comes from a Sioux Indian word that means "Sky water."

Fun Laws: 😂
• The land of 10,000 lakes declares mosquitos a public nuisance.
• It is illegal to stand around any building without a good reason to be there.

Good to know!
• The Mall of America in Minneapolis is one of the biggest malls in the world. It covers the same ground as 78 football fields!
• Another nickname for the state is the Land of 10,000 Lakes. There are so many rivers and lakes that 1 out of 6 Minnesotans owns a boat.
• Minneapolis has a skyway system connecting buildings which allows you to go all over town without ever going outside.

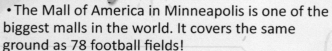

The most important inland waterway in the USA is the Mississippi River.

State Flower: Magnolia Blossom

Blues Birthplace. Mississippi Delta blues, also known as Delta blues, is a regional style of early 20th-century American folk music, centered in the Delta region of northwestern Mississippi.

"The W." The Mississippi University for Women was the first public women's college in the United States.

Did you know that **the Teddy Bear** was invented in honor of President Theodore Roosevelt? It all began after he refused to shoot a bear during a Mississippi hunting trip in November 1902.

Biloxi processes shrimp and other local fish. About 60 million pounds of shrimp are processed by them here every year.

Belzoni produces more than 350 million pounds of catfish a year. No wonder it's called the Catfish Capital of the World!

State Bird: Mockingbird

TENNESSEE

ARKANSAS

Tallahatchie River

Woodall Mt. 806 ft.

Tupelo•

Mississippi River

Tombigbee River

Yazoo River

Big Black River

Columbus•

•Greenville

•Belzoni

Meridian•

JACKSON

Vicksburg

Chickasawhay River

R E D   H I L L

ALABAMA

Pearl River

Leaf River

•Natchez

LOUISIANA

Pascagoula River

Biloxi•

GULF OF MEXICO

MISSISSIPPI/MS

WELCOME TO THE MAGNOLIA STATE

The Basics:
Total area: 48,432 sq. mi (125,438 sq. km)
Land area: 46,923 sq. mi (121,531 sq. km)
Population: 2,984,100
Capital: Jackson

STORY TO KNOW

Mississippi became the twentieth state in 1817 after hundreds of years of Spanish and French colonization. Its primary industries of cotton and slavery allowed it to flourish in the nation's early days, but it fell on hard times after the Civil War and the failure of secession. In many parts of the state, cotton, poultry, soybeans, and other agriculture still form the primary economy, and poverty is widespread. Nonetheless, the state marches on with a determination that only the South can muster.

The Mississippi River is famous around the world as the longest river in North America: it flows for 2,340 miles through ten states before emptying in to the Gulf of Mexico. This creates the fertile soil along its banks on which the magnolias, giving the "Magnolia State" its name, grow. And all along this great river are landmarks of the Civil Rights movement from the mid-twentieth century. Indeed, the whole state is steeped in history, right from the beginnings of slavery to modern-day civil liberties movements. Finally, like much of the south, Mississippi is famed for its cuisine — a visit is not complete without a dish of catfish and deep fried pickles.

The State Motto: "BY VALOR AND ARMS"

The Facts: 😎
Mississippi became the 20th state on December 10, 1817.
Major cities: Jackson, Gulfport, Hattiesburg, Southaven, Biloxi
Border states: Alabama, Arkansas, Louisiana, Tennessee

How Mississippi got its name: 😃
Mississippi comes from a Native American word meaning "Great river."

Fun Laws: 😄
• No one may bribe any athlete to "rig" a game, match, tournament, etc.

Good to know! 💡
• The first human lung transplant and heart transplant were performed at the University of Mississippi Medical Center.
• The cotton capital of the world is Greenwood, Mississippi.
• The longest man-made beach in the world is on the Mississippi Gulf Coast.

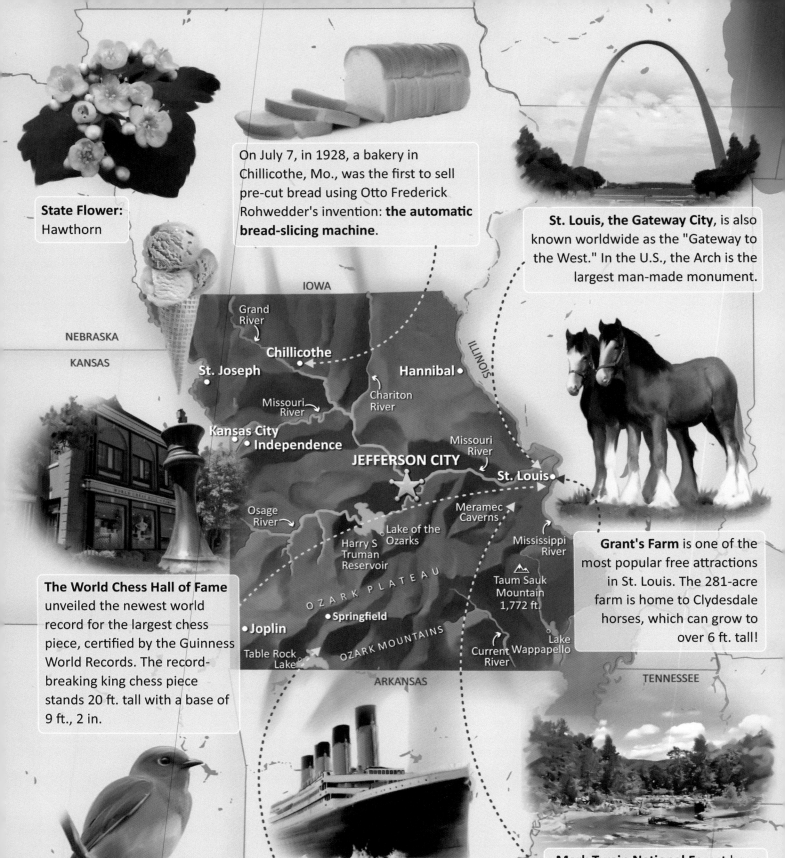

State Flower: Hawthorn

On July 7, in 1928, a bakery in Chillicothe, Mo., was the first to sell pre-cut bread using Otto Frederick Rohwedder's invention: **the automatic bread-slicing machine.**

St. Louis, the Gateway City, is also known worldwide as the "Gateway to the West." In the U.S., the Arch is the largest man-made monument.

IOWA

Grand River

NEBRASKA

KANSAS

Chillicothe

St. Joseph

Hannibal

ILLINOIS

Chariton River

Missouri River

Kansas City

Independence

JEFFERSON CITY

Missouri River

St. Louis

The World Chess Hall of Fame unveiled the newest world record for the largest chess piece, certified by the Guinness World Records. The record-breaking king chess piece stands 20 ft. tall with a base of 9 ft., 2 in.

Osage River

Harry S Truman Reservoir

Lake of the Ozarks

Meramec Caverns

Mississippi River

Taum Sauk Mountain 1,772 ft.

OZARK PLATEAU

Joplin

Springfield

Lake Wappapello

Table Rock Lake

OZARK MOUNTAINS

Current River

ARKANSAS

TENNESSEE

Grant's Farm is one of the most popular free attractions in St. Louis. The 281-acre farm is home to Clydesdale horses, which can grow to over 6 ft. tall!

State Bird: Bluebird

The Titanic Museum. Be ready to spend about 2 hours touring the museum, because the replica ship here is half the size of the original.

Mark Twain National Forest has a wide range of popular recreation opportunities. The forest has over 750 miles of trails for hiking, horseback riding, mountain biking, and motorized use.

MISSOURI/MO

WELCOME TO THE SHOW ME STATE

The Basics:
Total area: 69,707 sq. mi (180,540 sq. km)
Land area: 68,742 sq. mi (178,040 sq. km)
Population: 6,113,500
Capital: Jefferson City

STORY TO KNOW

Missouri was another state acquired through the Louisiana Purchase in 1803. In its early days, the land was explored by Lewis and Clark, and the region served as a staging ground between the East and West for decades during the 1800s, giving early pioneers a starting point on their journeys along the Santa Fe and Oregon trails. Today, this history as a gateway to the west is represented by the world's tallest monument: The Gateway Arch in St. Louis, towering at 630 feet tall. This city, and its rival across the river, Kansas City, are modern centers for transportation, manufacturing, and finance.

With the Ozarks in the South and the forest parks in the city, Missouri sees tourists year-round, whether they are looking for caves, rivers, forests, or rugged mountains. Country music lovers also have a home here, in Branson, where over 50 theaters put on shows ranging from music to magic to comedy, seating more people than Broadway! Crops in the form of cotton and rice also shore up the Show Me State's economy, with farmers throughout the state raising cattle, hogs, and poultry and growing corn and soybeans.

The State Motto: "THE WELFARE OF THE PEOPLE SHALL BE THE SUPREME LAW"

The Facts: 😎
Missouri became the 24th state on August 10, 1821.
Major cities: Kansas City, St. Louis, Springfield, Independence, Columbia, Lee's Summit
Border states: Kansas, Nebraska, Iowa, Illinois, Kentucky, Tennessee, Arkansas, Oklahoma

How Missouri got its name: 😜
Missouri comes from a Native American word that means "Big canoe river."

Fun Laws: 😂 😂
• Installation of bathtubs with four legs resembling animal paws is prohibited in Kansas City, MO.

Good to know! 💡
• The ice cream cone was invented at the World's Fair in St. Louis when an ice cream vendor ran out of cups and tried to use waffles instead.
• The first successful parachute jump from an airplane was made in St. Louis in 1912 by Captain Albert Berry. Iced tea was also invented at the World's Fair.
• Missouri is bordered by eight states.

Glacier National Park goes big in Montana – the park itself covers 1,583 sq. mi. and includes 762 lakes, more than 700 miles of hiking trails, 563 streams, 175 mountains (the highest of which is Mt. Cleveland at 10,448 ft.), and 25 glaciers (the largest of which has an area of 0.7 sq. mi.).

Wheat is Montana's leading cash crop. Montana is third among the wheat-producing states in the U.S. Wheat is grown in nearly all the counties in Montana, on more than 8950 wheat farms.

State Flower: Bitterroot

CANADA

Milk River

Missouri River

Flathead Lake

CONTINENTAL DIVIDE

ROCKY MOUNTAINS

• **Great Falls**

Fort Peck Lake

HELENA

Musselshell River

IDAHO

Missoula

Yellowstone River

NORTH DAKOTA

• **Butte**

SOUTH DAKOTA

Billings•

• **Bozeman**

Madison River   Granite Peak 12,799 ft.

WYOMING

Almost every Montana town has a rodeo.

The Garden of One Thousand Buddhas is both a spiritual refuge place and a Nyingma School of Tibetan Buddhism.

Evel Knievel

Evel Knievel was an American daredevil who became an icon in the 1970s for his incredible motorcycle stunts. He attempted more than 75 ramp-to-ramp motorcycle jumps. Some of the more famous among these include flying over the fountain at Caesars Palace in Las Vegas, jumping over busses, and many more.

The Mountain named "Froze-to-Death" is said to derive from the experiences of the local Crow tribe of Native Americans. The area can be deadly for unprepared visitors. Its rocky, broken terrain is difficult for travelers and snow is possible at any time of the year.

State Bird: Meadowlark

MONTANA/MT

WELCOME TO THE TREASURE STATE

The Basics:
Total area: 147,040 sq. mi (380,831 sq. km)
Land area: 145,546 sq. mi (376,962 sq. km)
Population: 1,050,500
Capital: Helena

STORY TO KNOW

The plains and mountains of Montana were home to many of the now most-famous Native American tribes in the New World. The Lakota and Cheyenne warriors soundly defeated the American Lt. Col. George Custer in the infamous Battle of Little Bighorn. This battle was part of the larger Sioux War, which had been precipitated when gold and silver discoveries attracted many new settlers to Montana in the mid-19th century. Today, Native Americans still make up 6 percent of the state's population, though the Sioux War was eventually won by the American settlers.

Today, Montana is known for its rugged beauty – it's home to Glacier National Park and parts of Yellowstone National Park, which it shares with Idaho and Wyoming. These parks, and the splendor of the rest of the state, make Montana one of the most beautiful areas of the country, and its people take great pride in their environment. It is often referred to as the "Last Best Place" on account of its millions of acres of pristine, untouched wilderness. Besides tourism, their primary industries are mining, timber, service, and agriculture.

The State Motto: "GOLD AND SILVER"

The Facts: 😎
Montana became the 41st state on November 8, 1889.
Major cities: Billings, Missoula, Great Falls, Bozeman, Butte, Helena
Border states: Wyoming, Idaho, South Dakota, North Dakota

How Montana got its name: 😜
The name Montana is a Spanish word that means "Mountainous."

Fun Laws: 😄 😄
• In Montana, it is illegal for married women to go fishing alone on Sundays, and illegal for unmarried women to fish alone at all.

Good to know! 💡
• Three of the five entrances to Yellowstone National Park are in Montana.
• The state is full of wildlife. The elk, deer and antelope populations all outnumber the humans.
• Montana is rich in deposits of copper, silver, and gold. This is how it got the name the Treasure State.

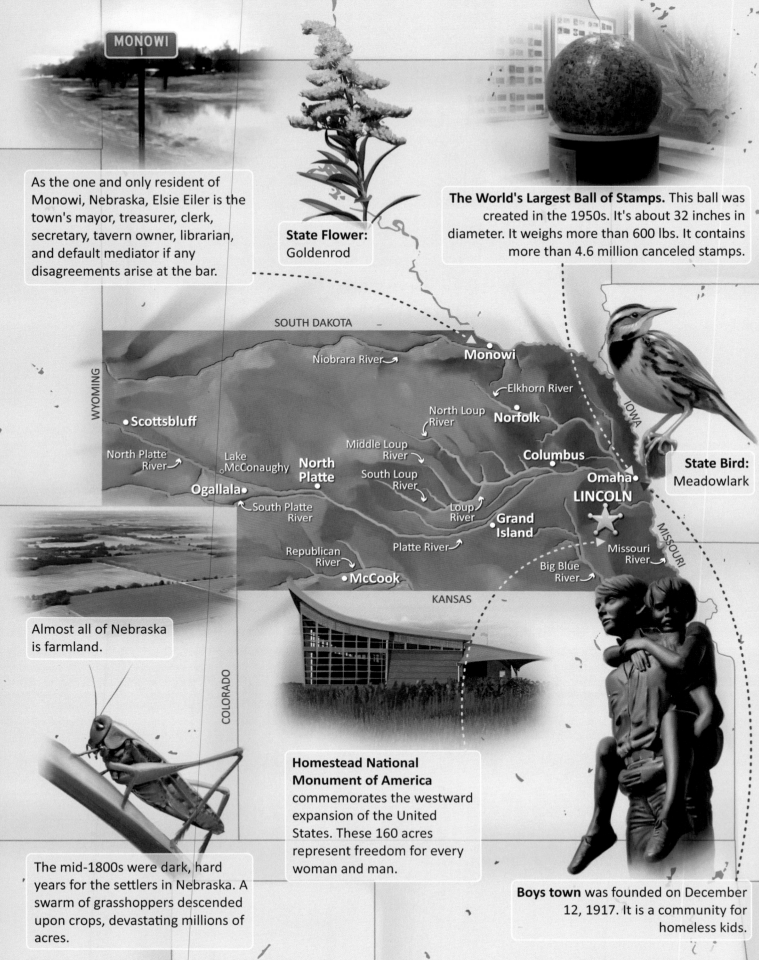

As the one and only resident of Monowi, Nebraska, Elsie Eiler is the town's mayor, treasurer, clerk, secretary, tavern owner, librarian, and default mediator if any disagreements arise at the bar.

State Flower: Goldenrod

The World's Largest Ball of Stamps. This ball was created in the 1950s. It's about 32 inches in diameter. It weighs more than 600 lbs. It contains more than 4.6 million canceled stamps.

SOUTH DAKOTA

Niobrara River

WYOMING

Monowi

Elkhorn River

North Loup River

Norfolk

Scottsbluff

Middle Loup River

Columbus

IOWA

North Platte River

Lake McConaughy

North Platte

South Loup River

Omaha

State Bird: Meadowlark

Ogallala

South Platte River

Loup River

LINCOLN

Grand Island

MISSOURI

Republican River

Platte River

Missouri River

Big Blue River

McCook

KANSAS

Almost all of Nebraska is farmland.

COLORADO

Homestead National Monument of America commemorates the westward expansion of the United States. These 160 acres represent freedom for every woman and man.

The mid-1800s were dark, hard years for the settlers in Nebraska. A swarm of grasshoppers descended upon crops, devastating millions of acres.

Boys town was founded on December 12, 1917. It is a community for homeless kids.

NEBRASKA/NE

WELCOME TO THE CORNHUSKER STATE

The Basics:
Total area: 77,348 sq. mi (200,330 sq. km)
Land area: 76,824 sq. mi (198,974 sq. km)
Population: 1,920,100
Capital: Lincoln

STORY TO KNOW

One of only a handful of states entering the union in the post-Civil War years, Nebraska was for centuries left to the Native Americans. Here, they would hunt bison, grow crops like corn, beans, pumpkins, and squash, and foray into the high passes above the North Platte River. Modern settlement was inevitable, though, and eventually ranchers and white colonies did move in. Today, the state is almost entirely covered in agriculture. From soybeans to wheat and corn, much of the farmland is fed through the vast Ogallala Aquifer underground, as well as from the Missouri River in regions where this flow.

Omaha is Nebraska's largest city, and it also serves as a financial center and a hub for insurance and agribusiness. Lincoln is the state's capital, with the only one-house legislature in the country. This Midwest state is a quiet place, and its people are friendly and warm. Famous Nebraskans include Gerald Ford, Marlon Brando, and Fred Astaire, but the state has been called home by many more artists, athletes, scientists, and politicians. Its natural beauty is unrivalled, with the world-famous Chimney Rock serving as an important landmark for travelers in the past and an important tourist destination for visitors today.

The State Motto: "EQUALITY BEFORE THE LAW"

The Facts: 😎
Nebraska became the 37th state on March 1, 1867.
Major cities: Omaha, Lincoln, Bellevue, Grand Island, Kearney, Fremont
Border states: Iowa, South Dakota, Wyoming, Colorado, Kansas, Missouri

How Nebraska got its name: 😜
Nebraska comes from the name The Oto Indians gave to the Platte River. It means "Flat water."

Fun Laws: 😄
• Drivers on mountains should drive with caution near the right-hand edge of the highway —There are no mountains in Nebraska!
• Doughnut holes may not be sold in Leigh, NE.

Good to know! 💡
• Nebraska is said to have more miles of river than any other state.
• The largest remaining area of original native prairie in the United States is in the Sand Hills region. It is an important stopover for migrating sand hill cranes.
• Spam, the food, is produced in Fremont, Nebraska.

The Fly Geyser is an unusual (and unplanned) collaboration between man and nature. The multi-colored geothermal geyser constantly sprays water five feet in the air!

State Flower:
Sagebrush

OREGON

IDAHO

State Bird:
Mountain Bluebird

Great Basin National Park. Almost anywhere in the park will provide you with beautiful views of the night sky. You can see the Milky Way pristinely from here.

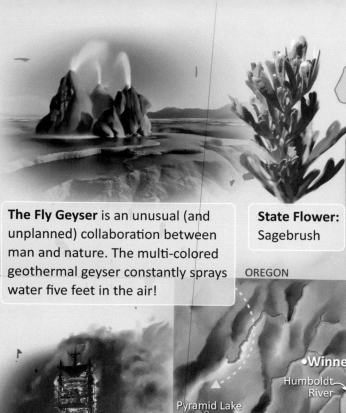

• Winnemucca

Humboldt River

• Elko

Pyramid Lake

SHOSHONE MOUNTAINS

RUBY MOUNTAINS

SNAKE MOUNTAINS

• Reno

Carson River

CARSON CITY

• Virginia City

Lake Tahoe

GREAT BASIN

EGAN MOUNTAINS

Red Rock Canyon State Park features scenic desert cliffs, buttes, and spectacular rock formations. Each tributary canyon is unique, with dramatic shapes and vivid colors.

Burning Man is an annual, week-long art festival in the Nevada desert where a 40-foot figure is burned!

Walker Lake

Boundary Peak 13,140 ft.

CALIFORNIA

MEADOW VALLEY WASH

UTAH

AREA 51

Lake Mead

NATIONAL RECREATION AREA

Las Vegas•

Colorado River

ARIZONA

The Nevada desert was the site for nuclear testing in the 1940s and 50s.

WELCOME TO Fabulous LAS VEGAS NEVADA

AREA 51

PACIFIC OCEAN

Las Vegas is the Entertainment Capital of the World. It is located in the Mojave Desert of Southern Nevada, and it's a desert metropolis built on gambling, parties, and other forms of entertainment.

Topping out at 726 ft. above the canyon floor and stretching 1,244 ft. across Black Canyon, **the Hoover Dam** was the tallest dam in the world when it opened in the 1930s. The Hoover Dam is an "arch-gravity" dam, which means it's thicker at the bottom (660 ft. thick, to be exact) and thinner at the top (where it's only 45 ft. thick).

NEVADA / NV

WELCOME TO THE SILVER STATE

The Basics:
Total area: 110,572 sq. mi (286,380 sq. km)
Land area: 109,781 sq. mi (284,332 sq. km)
Population: 2,998,000
Capital: Carson City

STORY TO KNOW

The original Nevada Territory was created in 1861, and it attained statehood only three years later. This was largely due to the discovery of gold and silver in the region, leading to a mining boom that helped propel Nevada into initial prosperity. Today, though, the landscape is dotted with ghost towns, the rise and fall of which were in lockstep with the discovery and depletion of these precious minerals. Native American tribes were a challenge to settlers as well, leading some to pass over the state and continue west. Nonetheless, it still thrives today, despite mining playing a much smaller role in the economy than it used to.

The 36th state is home to many of America's most well-known landmarks and places. Las Vegas is obviously the most famous, with its casinos, hotels, and entertainment, but there's also Reno, the Hoover Dam, and Area 51, a top-secret air force base north of Las Vegas. This state is one of the top tourist destinations in the entire world, with over 41 million people passing through every year! Although water problems face the state and will likely grow with time, this desert state still has much to offer its people and its many visitors.

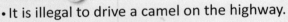

The State Motto: "ALL FOR OUR COUNTRY"

The Facts: 😎
Nevada became the 36th state on October 31, 1864.
Major cities: Las Vegas, Henderson, Reno, Sunrise Manor, Paradise, Spring Valley
Border states: Oregon, Idaho, Utah, Arizona, California

How Nevada got its name: 🤪
The name Nevada comes from a Spanish word that means "Snow-covered."

Fun Laws: 😄
• It is illegal to drive a camel on the highway.

Good to know! 💡
• Area 51, the place famed for UFO cover-ups, is located in southern Nevada.
• It is the driest state in the USA averaging only around 7 in. of rain each year.
• The state produces more gold than any other state in America.

State Bird: Purple Finch

A trip on an aerial tramway might just be the most spectacular seven minutes you spend in New Hampshire. The 80-passenger cable tram leaves every fifteen minutes to bring visitors up to Cannon Mountain's 4,080-foot summit.

Mount Washington, a mountain in the Presidential Range, is the highest (6,288 ft) peak of the White Mountains, in New Hampshire, U.S.A. The peak is 23 miles north-northwest of Conway. It is noted for its extreme weather conditions, one of the world's highest wind velocities (231 miles per hour) having been recorded there in 1934.

The Old Man of the Mountain has been an icon in the state of New Hampshire for many years, remaining so even after its fall in 2003.

The Christa McAuliffe Planetarium is a museum that bears the name of a Concord High School teacher, who tragically perished in the Space Shuttle Challenger explosion.

New Hampshire is a popular skiing and snowboarding destination thanks to the White Mountains. Ski jumping is a high school sport in this state!

The 800,000-acre White Mountains National Forest is a powerful presence. Forest covers 80% of New Hampshire's landscape.

State Flower: Purple Lilac

Map labels:
CANADA
VERMONT
WHITE MOUNTAINS
Androscoggin River
Berlin
Profile Mountain
Mt. Washington 6,288 ft.
MAINE
Pemigewasset River
Swift River
Connecticut River
Squam Lake
Merrimack River
Lake Winnipesaukee
CONCORD
Portsmouth
ATLANTIC OCEAN
Manchester
Keene
Nashua
MASSACHUSETTS
THE CHRISTA McAULIFFE PLANETARIUM

NEW HAMPSHIRE/NH

WELCOME TO THE GRANITE STATE

The Basics:
Total area: 9,349 sq. mi (24,214 sq. km)
Land area: 8,953 sq. mi (23,187 sq. km)
Population: 1,342,800
Capital: Concord

STORY TO KNOW

"Live free or die," is New Hampshire's motto, hearkening back to the Revolutionary War, when it became the very first colony to declare its independence from colonial Britain. After the war, it was the ninth state to ratify the U.S. constitution. As the centuries passed, New Hampshire transitioned from farming in the interior and sawmills and shipyards nearer the coast to modern, high-tech companies today. It still retains much of its industrial heritage despite these transitions, with manufacturing a key component of its economy even today.

In addition to its high-tech and manufacturing industries, the Granite State is awash in tourism. Boasting mountains, rivers, ocean, fall foliage, lakes, and more, tourists from both inside and outside the state have good reason to travel throughout New Hampshire any time of year. Hunting, skiing, fishing, and hiking are just a few of the activities you can enjoy while taking in the spectacular natural landscapes of the state. All of this has made New Hampshire home to a great number of US Olympians, bringing home medals with considerable success for a state of its size. Whatever your reason, a visit to New Hampshire is not one you'll soon forget!

The State Motto: "LIVE FREE OR DIE"

The Facts: 🤓
New Hampshire became the 9th state on June 21, 1788.
Major cities: Manchester, Nashua, Concord, Derry
Border states: Vermont, Maine, Massachusetts

How New Hampshire got its name: 😄
New Hampshire was named by Captain John Mason after a city in England named Hampshire.

Fun Laws: 😂
• You may not tap your feet, nod your head, or in any way keep time to the music in a tavern, restaurant, or cafe.

Good to know! 💡
• New Hampshire was the first state to have its own state constitution.
• The top of Mt. Washington in New Hampshire is said to have the worst weather on earth. A world record for wind speed was clocked here at 231 miles per hour!
• Christa McAuliffe was a high school teacher Christa McAuliffe and the first American civilian selected to go into space. She died in the explosion of the space shuttle "Challenger" in 1986.

State Flower: Violet

The Sterling Hill Mine is a former iron and zinc mine. There, you can find a great variety of huge, fluorescent minerals.

The Garden State is famous for its Jersey tomatoes.

PENNSYLVANIA

NEW YORK

APPALACHIAN MOUNTAINS

Hackensack River

Lake Hopatcong

Passaic River

Hudson River

Musconetcong River

Newark•

•**Hoboken**
•**Jersey City**

PIEDMONT PLATEAU

New Jersey designated **Hadrosaurus foulkii** as its official state dinosaur in 1991 because it was the first dinosaur discovered in North America.

•**Princeton**

TRENTON

Toms River

Delaware River

•**Camden**
•**Haddonfield**

George Washington Bridge, a vehicular suspension bridge crossing the Hudson River, lies between The Palisades park near Fort Lee and Manhattan island, containing 43,000 tons of steel!

Mullica River

Great Egg Harbor River

Jersey Shore Resorts

Atlantic city•

DELAWARE

DELAWARE BAY

Cape May is a paradise for beach lovers. Also, it's famous for its antique architecture and old-fashioned charm.

•Cape May

Atlantic City Boardwalk

State Bird: Goldfinch

ATLANTIC OCEAN

NEW JERSEY/NJ

WELCOME TO THE GARDEN STATE

The Basics:
Total area: 8,723 sq. mi (22,591 sq. km)
Land area: 7,354 sq. mi (19,047 sq. km)
Population: 9,005,600
Capital: Trenton

STORY TO KNOW

As the third U.S. state and the first to sign the Bill of Rights, New Jersey is rightfully one of the most well-known states around the world. It saw more than 90 battles in the Revolutionary War, making it a highly war-torn region in the ensuing years. Throughout the later centuries, northern New Jersey saw rapid industrialization, while the southern portion developed into a thriving agricultural center, earning it the nickname "Garden State". Today, these parallel industries remain much the same, and New Jersey is home to enormous regions of cranberry farm.

Large, complex highway and rail systems make New Jersey a hub for the entire Atlantic Seaboard, and its many large cities have as much to offer as any major American metropolis. It's also home to Ivy League schools like Princeton, and the state sees tourists who visit the Jersey Shore and its other beaches regularly. Don't let its small size fool you — New Jersey is the most densely populated state in the entire country. Its people and its rich cultural heritage are unique and colorful, which you'll soon learn upon visiting!

The State Motto: "LIBERTY AND PROSPERITY"

The Facts: 🤓
New Jersey became the 3rd state on December 18, 1787.
Major cities: Newark, Jersey City, Paterson, Elizabeth, Edison, Woodbridge
Border states: Delaware, Pennsylvania, New York

How New Jersey got its name: 🤪
New Jersey was named after the British island of Jersey in the English Channel, off the coast of Normandy. The name was chosen in honor of one of the region's founders, Sir George Carteret, who was from Jersey.

Fun Laws: 😄 😄
• You may not slurp your soup.

Good to know! 💡
• Over 100 battles have been fought on New Jersey soil.
• New Jersey is a state of inventions. The FM Radio, the light bulb, the motion picture camera, and transistors were all invented in New Jersey.
• The Atlantic City Boardwalk was the world's first boardwalk.

UTAH

Aztec Ruins National Monument, an archaeological site in northwestern New Mexico. This national monument was established in 1923 and designated a World Heritage site in 1987. It has an area of about 320 acres.

State Flower: Yucca

The Albuquerque International Balloon Fiesta is the largest balloon event in the world. Held each year during the first week in October, the Balloon Fiesta now attracts almost 600 balloons and 1000 pilots.

COLORADO

OKLAHOMA

• **Farmington**

San Juan River

Wheeler Peak 13,161 ft.

• **Taos**

Canadian River

Chaco Culture National Historic Park

Coyote •

Los Alamos •

SANTA FE

• **Gallup**

CONTINENTAL DIVIDE

• **Albuquerque**

The best chilis in the world are grown in the fertile Hatch and Rio Grande Valleys in New Mexico. The state grows more than 50,000 tons of chilis annually.

Rio Grande

Lincoln National Forest

ROCKY MOUNTAINS

Pecos River

Clovis •

International UFO Museum and Research Center. Museum exhibits include information on the Roswell Incident, crop circles, UFO sightings, Area 51, ancient astronauts, and abductions.

• **Mogollon**

Glia River

Roswell •

• **Silver City**

• **Las Cruces**

Carlsbad Caverns

ARIZONA

• **Columbus**

TEXAS

MEXICO

The largest gypsum dune field in the world is located at **White Sands National Monument** in south-central New Mexico.

State Bird: Roadrunner

Carlsbad Caverns is one of the oldest and most famous cave systems in the world. From about mid-April to late-October, thousands of bats fly out of Carlsbad Cavern every evening, weather permitting, to eat insects.

NEW MEXICO / NM

WELCOME TO THE COLORFUL STATE

The Basics:
Total area: 121,590 sq. mi (314,917 sq. km)
Land area: 121,298 sq. mi (314,161 sq. km)
Population: 2,088,100
Capital: Santa Fe

STORY TO KNOW

A decade before the Mayflower had even reached America, the Spanish had already founded Santa Fe in New Mexico – this stands today as the oldest European-founded capital in the country. This state, one of the very last to join the nation, is situated in the dry desert Southwest, and is actually the driest state in America. Only 0.002% of its total area is comprised of rivers or lakes! The region is nonetheless steeped in history and culture. Ancestral Puebloan sites, archaeology digs, dinosaur remains, and spectacular sandstone ruins can be found all over the state, many located within the Chaco Culture National Historical Park.

The rugged natural beauty of New Mexico is also a sight to behold. The state is split by the Rocky Mountains, and it is also home to the Carlsbad Caverns in the Guadalupe range. The mesas and canyons of New Mexico are renowned for their pristine and awe-inspiring splendor, and the residents know it. From farmers to miners to oil and gas, the primary industries have people of many walks of life living here, creating an interesting mixture of Hispanic, European, and Native American influence on the New Mexico lifestyle. Whether you're visiting Albuquerque or looking for a solitary desert experience, the state has something to offer you!

The State Motto: "IT GROWS AS IT GOES"

The Facts: 🤓
New Mexico became the 47th state on January 6, 1912.
Major cities: Albuquerque, Las Cruces, Rio Rancho, Santa Fe, Roswell
Border states: Colorado, Utah, Arizona, Texas, Oklahoma

How New Mexico got its name: 😜
The region was named by the first Spanish settlers in the area after the country of Mexico to the south.

Fun Laws: 😆
• Idiots may not vote.

Good to know! 💡
• The real Smokey Bear was rescued from a New Mexico fire in 1950.
• New Mexico is one of the four states that meet at the Four Corners. You can stand in four states at the same time! The other three states are Colorado, Utah, and Arizona.
• There are more cattle and sheep in the state than people.

The **Adirondack Mountains** are home to a vast number of deciduous tree species – the kind that change colors in the fall and shed their leaves in the winter. You can see very colorful results!

State Bird:
Bluebird

VERMONT

Did you know that **Syracuse is the snowiest big city in the entire United States**? Syracuse experiences the highest average snowfall of any American city!

CANADA

LAKE ONTARIO

Lake Champlain

Thousand Islands

Lake Placid

Mt. Marcy 5,344 ft.

ADIRONDACK MOUNTAINS

Lake George

Oneida Lake

Mohawk River

•Rochester Syracuse Utica•

CANADA

Niagara Falls

•**Buffalo**
•**East Aurora**

LAKE ERIE

Finger Lakes

Cooperstown

Susquehanna River

ALBANY

CATSKILL MOUNTAINS

Hudson River

MA

"**The Statue of Liberty Enlightening the World**" was a gift of friendship from the people of France to the United States and is recognized as a universal symbol of freedom and democracy. The Statue of Liberty was dedicated on October 28, 1886.

Elmira•

Binghamton•

PENNSYLVANIA

CT

West Point

Long Island Sound

Niagara Falls is a world-famous waterfall that straddles the international border between Canada and the US. The Falls at Niagara are about 12,000 years old.

Cooperstown is home to **the National Baseball Hall of Fame and Museum.**

Long Island

•**New York City**
Staten Island

ATLANTIC OCEAN

State Flower:
Rose

Coney Island is a New York City neighborhood that features an amusement area that includes 50 or more separate rides and attractions.

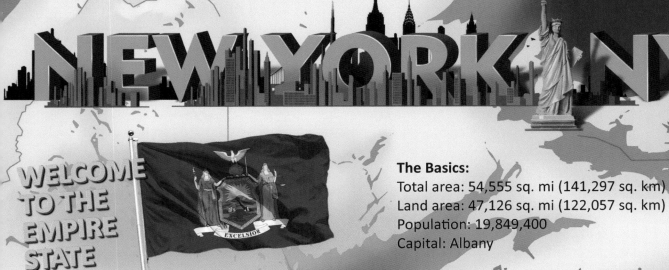

NEW YORK · NY

WELCOME TO THE EMPIRE STATE

The Basics:
Total area: 54,555 sq. mi (141,297 sq. km)
Land area: 47,126 sq. mi (122,057 sq. km)
Population: 19,849,400
Capital: Albany

STORY TO KNOW

While it stands as a cultural and urban capital in its own right, New York, New York was in fact the actual first capital of the United States, and George Washington was sworn in on the steps of its Federal Hall. And although the city is obviously known in every corner of the globe for its people, its towering buildings (including the Statue of Liberty!), its pizza, its diversity, and its fast-paced atmosphere, the state of New York itself is home to much more than just the nation's largest metropolis (clocking in at 8 million people – more than the populations of 40 US states in their entirety!).

Outside the city that never sleeps, New York is home to the parts of the Appalachians, to cities with small-town feels like Ithaca and the state capital of Albany, to Ivy League universities such as Cornell, to expansive pine forests, and a rugged natural coastline. Natural wonders like Niagara Falls or the Adirondacks are never far away. Other large cities, including Buffalo and Rochester, also serve as industrial giants alongside their larger counterpart. And finally, shared borders with New Jersey, Connecticut, and Pennsylvania, all of which share urban regions with New York City, make the state an indispensable hub for industry and commerce of all kinds.

The State Motto: "EVER UPWARD"

The Facts: 🤓
New York became the 11th state on July 26, 1788.
Major cities: New York City, Buffalo, Rochester, Yonkers, Syracuse, Albany
Border states: Pennsylvania, New Jersey, Vermont, Massachusetts, Connecticut, Rhode Island (maritime border)

How New York got its name: 🤭
When the English took over the land from the Dutch, they named it New York in honor of the Duke of York and the city of York in England.

Fun Laws: 😄 😄
• It is against the law to throw a ball at someone's head for fun.

Good to know! 💡
• The New York City Subway is one of the largest subway systems in the world. It has 722 miles of track.
• Taxi cabs are yellow because the man who started the Yellow Cab company read that yellow is the easiest color to spot.
• The index finger of the Statue of Liberty is 8 ft. long.
• New York City was the capital of the United States from 1785 to 1790.

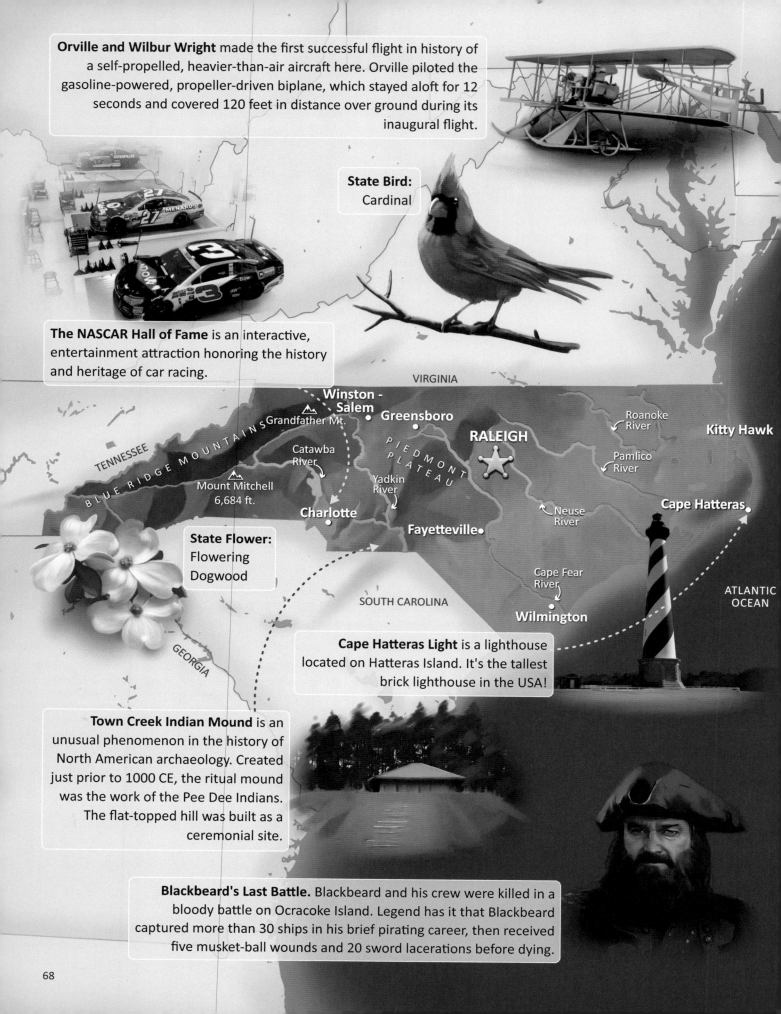

Orville and Wilbur Wright made the first successful flight in history of a self-propelled, heavier-than-air aircraft here. Orville piloted the gasoline-powered, propeller-driven biplane, which stayed aloft for 12 seconds and covered 120 feet in distance over ground during its inaugural flight.

State Bird:
Cardinal

The NASCAR Hall of Fame is an interactive, entertainment attraction honoring the history and heritage of car racing.

VIRGINIA

Winston - Salem
Grandfather Mt.
Greensboro
Roanoke River
Kitty Hawk

TENNESSEE
BLUE RIDGE MOUNTAINS
Catawba River
PIEDMONT PLATEAU
RALEIGH
Pamlico River

Mount Mitchell 6,684 ft.
Yadkin River

Charlotte
Neuse River
Cape Hatteras

State Flower:
Flowering Dogwood

Fayetteville

GEORGIA
SOUTH CAROLINA
Cape Fear River

ATLANTIC OCEAN

Wilmington

Cape Hatteras Light is a lighthouse located on Hatteras Island. It's the tallest brick lighthouse in the USA!

Town Creek Indian Mound is an unusual phenomenon in the history of North American archaeology. Created just prior to 1000 CE, the ritual mound was the work of the Pee Dee Indians. The flat-topped hill was built as a ceremonial site.

Blackbeard's Last Battle. Blackbeard and his crew were killed in a bloody battle on Ocracoke Island. Legend has it that Blackbeard captured more than 30 ships in his brief pirating career, then received five musket-ball wounds and 20 sword lacerations before dying.

NORTH CAROLINA/NC

WELCOME TO THE TAR HEEL STATE

The Basics:
Total area: 53,819 sq. mi (139,391 sq. km)
Land area: 48,618 sq. mi (125,920 sq. km)
Population: 10,273,400
Capital: Raleigh

STORY TO KNOW

The original Carolina colony was made up of modern-day North Carolina, South Carolina, and parts of Georgia. It wasn't until 1789 that the current state became the 12th in the country. During the Civil War, North Carolina seceded, and they provided more men, supplies, and equipment to the Confederacy than any other state. As with most Southern states, North Carolina was hit hard after their loss, but they've rebounded from their traditional industries of agriculture, textiles, and furniture-making to include research and other high-tech sectors.

College basketball, barbecue, and the Wright Brothers at Kitty Hawk are perhaps what North Carolina is most famous for, both in America and abroad. But while these are all great aspects of the state, it does have even more to offer! The Great Smoky Mountains, its little-known surfing spots, and the majesty of the Appalachia are all also on offer here. From Raleigh to Charlotte and everything in between, North Carolina truly embodies Southern Hospitality in all its many wonderful forms!

The State Motto: "TO BE, RATHER THAN TO SEEM TO BE"

The Facts: 🤓
North Carolina became the 12th state on November 21, 1789.
Major cities: Charlotte, Raleigh, Greensboro, Durham, Winston-Salem, Fayetteville
Border states: Virginia, Tennessee, Georgia, South Carolina

How North Carolina got its name: 😀
The name "Carolina" is given for King Charles, which is written "Carolus" in Latin.

Fun Laws: 😄
• It's against the law to sing off key.

Good to know!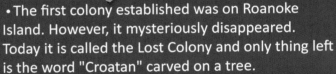
• The first colony established was on Roanoke Island. However, it mysteriously disappeared. Today it is called the Lost Colony and only thing left is the word "Croatan" carved on a tree.
• The first public university in the United States was the University of North Carolina.
• Virginia Dare was the first child born in America in Roanoke, North Carolina in 1587.
• North Carolina leads the USA in textile production.

Mystical Horizons. The so-called "Stonehenge of the prairie" has a breathtaking view overlooking farmland west of the Turtle Mountains. Stone and cement structures are designed to view summer and winter solstice and the equinox.

State Bird:
Meadowlark

The International Peace Garden is at the heart of the Turtle Mountains. It was established on July 14, 1932, as a symbol of the peaceful relationship between the U.S. and Canada.

CANADA

MONTANA

Souris River

Rugby

Red River

Minot•

Devils Lake

Grand Forks•

Lake Sakakawea

Garrison Dam

Little Missouri River

Knife River

Missouri River

Sheyenne River

Fargo•

RED RIVER VALLEY

BISMARCK

Jamestown•

Maple River

State Flower:
Wild Prairie Rose

Dickinson•

Heart River

James River

MINNESOTA

Cannonball River

White Butte 3,506 ft.

Theodore Roosevelt National Park. This park was named for the 26th U.S. President Theodore Roosevelt, who loved to ranch here. The National Park is comprised of three separate regions in western North Dakota.

SOUTH DAKOTA

Made up of 2,000 wheel rims, **the W'eel Turtle of Dunseith**, North Dakota, is arguably the largest turtle in the world.

The Geographic Center of North America lies in the town of Rugby. It's marked by a rock obelisk, about 15 ft. tall, marked by the flags of Canada, Mexico, and the U.S.

NORTH DAKOTA / ND

WELCOME TO THE PEACE GARDEN STATE

The Basics:
Total area: 70,698 sq. mi (183,108 sq. km)
Land area: 69,001 sq. mi (178,711 sq. km)
Population: 755,393
Capital: Bismarck

STORY TO KNOW

North Dakota is one of America's least-populated states – but not for lack of beauty or opportunity. This hidden gem contains vast tracts of pristine wilderness, and even its largest cities, such as Fargo, retain a small-town feel that has been lost in much of the country. This region was first visited by Lewis and Clark in the early 1800s, where they learned of the many Native American legends that abound in the area. It achieved statehood in 1889, one of the final states to do so (in conjunction with South Dakota), coming in at 39th.

From the Red River in the north, to the Missouri River and the Garrison Dam in the south, and from the vast wilderness of rolling hills to the wide prairies lush with agriculture, North Dakota is a jewel of wilderness in the United States. Theodore Roosevelt National Park allows you to see bison, elk, and wild horses roaming where they have for thousands of years, in pristine, untouched grasslands. The peaceful environment of North Dakota is what draws visitors year-round, and it's also what keeps residents living there happily and enjoyably.

The State Motto: "LIBERTY AND UNION, NOW AND FOREVER, ONE AND INSEPARABLE"

The Facts: 😎
North Dakota became the 39th state on November 2, 1889.
Major cities: Fargo, Bismarck, Grand Forks, Minot
Border states: Montana, South Dakota, Minnesota

How North Dakota got its name: 😃
The name Dakota comes from a Sioux Indian word for "Friend."

Fun Laws: 😄
• It is illegal to lie down and fall asleep with your shoes on.

Good to know! 💡
• North Dakota grows more sunflowers than any other US state.
• North Dakota was the first state to finish its portion of the Interstate Highway System.
• The official state beverage is milk.

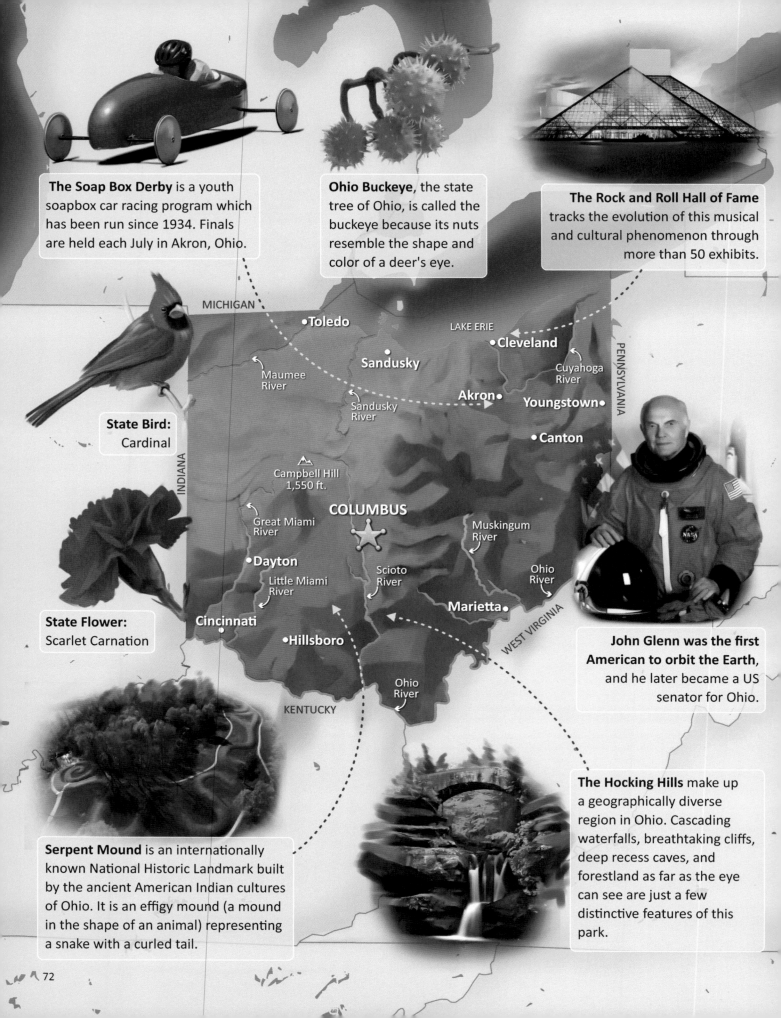

The Soap Box Derby is a youth soapbox car racing program which has been run since 1934. Finals are held each July in Akron, Ohio.

Ohio Buckeye, the state tree of Ohio, is called the buckeye because its nuts resemble the shape and color of a deer's eye.

The Rock and Roll Hall of Fame tracks the evolution of this musical and cultural phenomenon through more than 50 exhibits.

MICHIGAN

•Toledo

LAKE ERIE

•Cleveland

Sandusky

Cuyahoga River

Maumee River

Akron•

Youngstown•

PENNSYLVANIA

Sandusky River

State Bird:
Cardinal

•Canton

INDIANA

⛰ Campbell Hill 1,550 ft.

COLUMBUS

Great Miami River

Muskingum River

•Dayton

Scioto River

Ohio River

Little Miami River

State Flower:
Scarlet Carnation

Cincinnati

Marietta•

WEST VIRGINIA

•Hillsboro

John Glenn was the first American to orbit the Earth, and he later became a US senator for Ohio.

Ohio River

KENTUCKY

Serpent Mound is an internationally known National Historic Landmark built by the ancient American Indian cultures of Ohio. It is an effigy mound (a mound in the shape of an animal) representing a snake with a curled tail.

The Hocking Hills make up a geographically diverse region in Ohio. Cascading waterfalls, breathtaking cliffs, deep recess caves, and forestland as far as the eye can see are just a few distinctive features of this park.

OHIO/OH

WELCOME TO THE BUCKEYE STATE

The Basics:
Total area: 44,826 sq. mi (116,098 sq. km)
Land area: 40,861 sq. mi (105,829 sq. km)
Population: 11,658,600
Capital: Columbus

STORY TO KNOW

What's round on both ends and says "hi" in the middle? Ohio! This state became part of the US after the Revolutionary War, and even today it plays a key role in American politics. Many presidents have hailed from here, and its electoral votes have proved decisive in nearly every federal election in recent memory. Its manufacturing industries have long been mainstays of its economy, but its many cities, including Cincinnati, Toledo, Cleveland, and Columbus, are home to many, many industries. From music to education to government to finance, there are many ways to spend a life here.

Although steel, machinery, rubber, and other heavy industries have been dominant in Ohio, agriculture still plays a role in the state's western plains. Here, farmers grow soybeans and corn in the flat areas, carved out by glaciers in the last ice age. Innovators like Thomas Edison called Ohio home, and it has a reputation for its inventive people: The National Inventors Hall of Fame is here, with many modern innovations, like the cash register, the airplane, and even the hot dog having been created in the state! As America's once western frontier, Ohio remains today an important piece of the American cultural milieu.

The State Motto: "WITH GOD, ALL THINGS ARE POSSIBLE"

The Facts: 😎
Ohio became the 17th state on March 1, 1803.
Major cities: Columbus, Cleveland, Cincinnati, Toledo, Akron, Dayton
Border states: Michigan, Indiana, Kentucky, West Virginia, Pennsylvania

How Ohio got its name: 🤓
The name Ohio comes from a Native American Iroquois word meaning "Great river."

Fun Laws: 😄 😄
• It is illegal for more than five women to live in a house.

Good to know! 💡
• The first traffic light was in Cleveland, Ohio.
• Seven presidents of the United States were born in Ohio. They are Ulysses S. Grant, Rutherford Hayes, James Garfield, Benjamin Harrison, William McKinley, William Howard Taft, and Warren Harding.
• Neil Armstrong, the first man to walk on the moon, came from Ohio.

In 1935, **the first parking meter** was invented and installed in Oklahoma.

At one time, Tulsa, Oklahoma, sat atop the world's largest-known ocean of oil. Drilling derricks were everywhere, even on the lawn of the state capitol. The city called itself the **"Oil Capital of the World."**

The state monument, a 76-foot-tall statue of a bare-chested golden man with a belt reading "TULSA" on the buckle, is known as **the Golden Driller**. It is a 60-year-old monument to honor the workers of the petroleum industry.

COLORADO

KANSAS

MISSOURI

Black Mesa 4,973 ft.

North Canadian River

Cimarron River

Arkansas River

Oolagah Lake

NEW MEXICO

• Enid

Tulsa

Chisholm Trail

•Guthrie

OKLAHOMA CITY

Muskogee •

Washita River

Canadian River

State Bird: Scissor-tailed Flycatcher

WICHITA MOUNTAINS

OUACHITA MOUNTAINS

Wind energy is expanding in Oklahoma, especially in western parts of the state. More than 15 percent of the electricity generated in Oklahoma comes from this renewable source.

Red River

Lake Texoma

TEXAS

ARKANSAS

State Flower: Mistletoe (A tree parasite)

Toy and Action Figure Museum. This museum displays over 13,000 collectibles, moveable-joint heroes, villains, monsters, and accessories, many in their original packaging.

Southeastern Oklahoma is known for its scenery, and one of its most picturesque areas is **the Kiamichi Mountains**, with elevations reaching 2,500 feet above sea level. Local lore claims that Bigfoot lives here.

OKLAHOMA / OK

WELCOME TO THE SOONER STATE

OKLAHOMA

The Basics:
Total area: 69,899 sq. mi (181,037 sq. km)
Land area: 68,595 sq. mi (177,660 sq. km)
Population: 3,930,900
Capital: Oklahoma City

STORY TO KNOW

Oklahoma has a painful history for Native Americans, who were granted the land as Indian Territory in 1834 but had to travel along the brutal "Trail of Tears" to get there. By 1889, they were once again forced to contend with white settlement, as America had opened the region up for this, and finally Oklahoma became a bona fide state in 1907. Nonetheless, today it remains as the second-highest Native American populated state, and its home as the largest diversity of tribes in the entire country. For those that remain, and for the descendants of the white settlers who now also call the land home, industry abounds: after the Great Depression and the dustbowl conditions were past, agriculture, oil and natural gas, cattle, wheat, and iron all became core components of the Oklahoman economy.

Oklahoma City is a federal government headquarters, so there are many jobs in this sector available there. The cuisine has a distinctly southern influence, including fried okra, cornbread, biscuits, pork barbecue, and pecan pie! Outside of the cities, the state is home to beautiful scenery and rugged bluffs and valleys worth exploring for even the most seasoned adventurer. Rolling hills lead west to the High Plains in the state's panhandle. The windy prairies of the state are also now home to many wind farms, modernizing the state's industries and helping provide it with much-needed energy.

The State Motto: "LABOR CONQUERS ALL THINGS"

The Facts: 😎
Oklahoma became the 46th state on November 16, 1907.
Major cities: Oklahoma City, Tulsa, Norman, Broken Arrow, Lawton, Edmond
Border states: Texas, New Mexico, Colorado, Kansas, Missouri, Arkansas

How Oklahoma got its name: 😀
The name Oklahoma comes from two words in the Choctaw Indian language: "Okla," which means "People," and "Humma," which means "Red."

Fun Laws: 😄😄
• Dogs must have a permit signed by the mayor in order to congregate in groups of three or more on private property.

Good to know! 💡
• Oklahoma has the largest population of Native Americans of any state.
• The tribal capital of the Cherokee Nation is located in Tahlequah.
• The National Cowboy Hall of Fame and Museum is located in Oklahoma City.

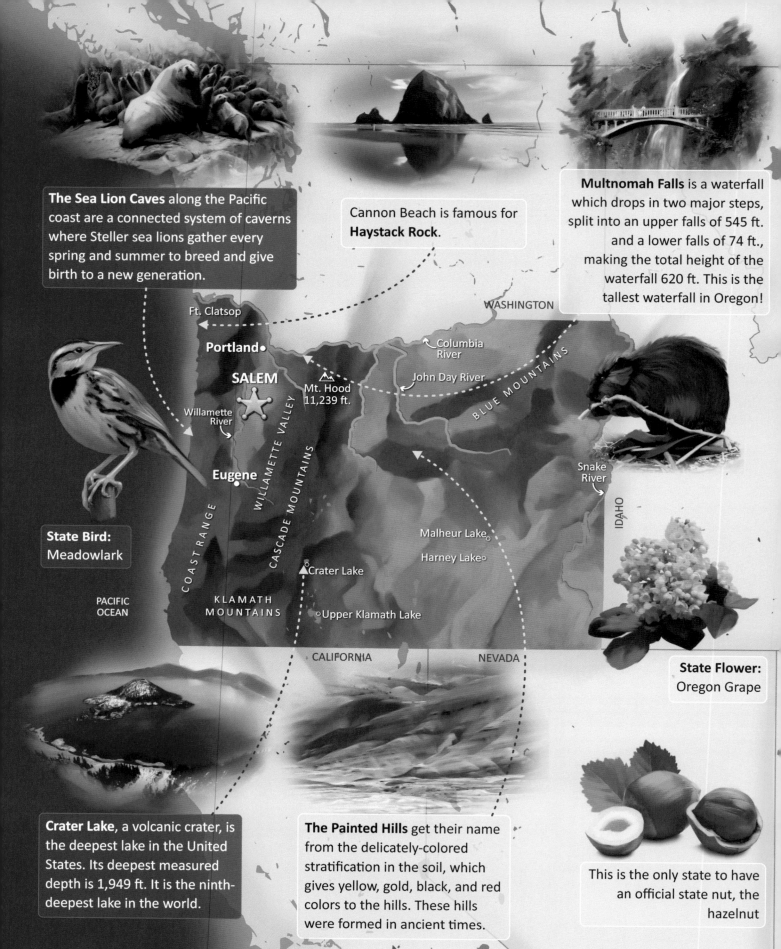

The Sea Lion Caves along the Pacific coast are a connected system of caverns where Steller sea lions gather every spring and summer to breed and give birth to a new generation.

Cannon Beach is famous for **Haystack Rock**.

Multnomah Falls is a waterfall which drops in two major steps, split into an upper falls of 545 ft. and a lower falls of 74 ft., making the total height of the waterfall 620 ft. This is the tallest waterfall in Oregon!

WASHINGTON

Ft. Clatsop

Portland•

SALEM

Columbia River

John Day River

Mt. Hood 11,239 ft.

BLUE MOUNTAINS

Willamette River

Eugene

WILLAMETTE VALLEY

CASCADE MOUNTAINS

COAST RANGE

Snake River

IDAHO

State Bird:
Meadowlark

Malheur Lake○

Harney Lake○

▲Crater Lake

PACIFIC OCEAN

KLAMATH MOUNTAINS

○Upper Klamath Lake

CALIFORNIA

NEVADA

State Flower:
Oregon Grape

Crater Lake, a volcanic crater, is the deepest lake in the United States. Its deepest measured depth is 1,949 ft. It is the ninth-deepest lake in the world.

The Painted Hills get their name from the delicately-colored stratification in the soil, which gives yellow, gold, black, and red colors to the hills. These hills were formed in ancient times.

This is the only state to have an official state nut, the hazelnut

OREGON / OR

WELCOME TO THE BEAVER STATE

STATE OF OREGON
1859

The Basics:
Total area: 98,379 sq. mi (254,799 sq. km)
Land area: 95,988 sq. mi (248,608 sq. km)
Population: 4,142,800
Capital: Salem

STORY TO KNOW

In the Pacific Northwest, Oregon stands as a jewel of natural beauty, with hundreds of miles of scenic coastline that see visitors from all over. Lush deciduous rainforest fills the northern parts of the state, and expansive sand dunes can be explored in the southwest. Rural and eastern Oregon are important agricultural regions for the state. Other industries, such as aluminum production and hydroelectricity generation, help provide a very diverse economy. The city of Portland is well-known for its culture, craft beers, coffee shops, and cycling! In fact, in 1971, Oregon passed a "Bicycle Bill," ensuring all future roads must include sections for bikes and pedestrians.

Oregon was first settled via the now-famous Oregon Trail. Long before this, though, the coast was home to many Native Americans, who survived heartily on the abundant fish and wildlife in the region. The Willamette Valley saw the first farming settlements, and eventually, after statehood in 1859, railroads that linked the state all the way back to the eastern seaboard were finally completed. Since then, industry and an appreciation for Oregon's natural beauty have been mainstays of the state.

The State Motto: "SHE FLIES WITH HER OWN WINGS"

The Facts: 🤓
Oregon became the 33rd state on February 14, 1859.
Major cities: Portland, Eugene, Salem, Gresham, Hillsboro, Beaverton
Border states: California, Nevada, Idaho, Washington

How Oregon got its name: 😛
No one is quite sure where the name Oregon comes from. It possibly came from the previous name for the Columbia River, The Ouragan. This was a French word that meant "Hurricane."

Fun Laws: 😂
• A door on a car may not be left open longer than is necessary.

Good to know! 💡
• The Oregon state flag has a beaver on the back. It is the only US state flag with a different image on the reverse side.
• At 1949 ft. deep, Crater Lake is the deepest lake in the United States.
• Oregon harvests more timber than any other state.
• Oregon has the most ghost towns of any state. Booooooo!

Philadelphia served as the temporary capital of the United States of America between 1790 and 1800 while Washington, D.C., was being built.

State Flower:
Mountain Laurel

Benjamin Franklin, printer and publisher, author, inventor, scientist, and diplomat, lived in Pennsylvania.

LAKE ERIE

•Erie

NEW YORK

OHIO

Allegheny River

West Susquehanna River

Scranton

ALLEGHENY MOUNTAINS

APPALACHIAN MOUNTAINS

Ohio River

Susquehanna River

Bethlehem•

Delaware River

NJ

Altoona

HARRISBURG

•Hershey

•Pittsburgh

•Johnstown

Juniata River

•Reading

Valley Forge

State Bird:
Ruffed Grouse

Monongahela River

Mt. Davis 3,213 ft.

Philadelphia•

•Gettysburg

DELAWARE

WEST VIRGINIA

MARYLAND

The Rocky Statue and the "Rocky Steps" are undeniably two of the most popular attractions in Philadelphia.

Independence National Park is known as the birthplace of American democracy. The Liberty Bell is also an iconic symbol of American independence.

The Constitution of the United States, the Declaration of Independence, and the Gettysburg Address were all written in Pennsylvania.

PENNSYLVANIA/PA

WELCOME TO THE KEYSTONE STATE

The Basics:
Total area: 46,054 sq. mi (119,280 sq. km)
Land area: 44,743 sq. mi (115,883 sq. km)
Population: 12,805,500
Capital: Harrisburg

STORY TO KNOW

One of the most historically significant states in the entire nation, Pennsylvania has been home to the Gettysburg address, key battles in the Revolutionary War, the Liberty Bell, and much more. This is the very birthplace of the constitution itself. As the central colony among the original thirteen, Pennsylvania provided its surrounding regions with stability and a political anchor. This was the very second state to join the Union, and Philadelphia served as the nation's capital for a time in the late 1700s.

Today, Philadelphia and Pittsburgh remain major urban centers, both in Pennsylvania and the United States as a whole. The state is also home to Ivy League universities, booming high-tech industries, and a robust tourism sector. Coal and steel are both key factors in the state's economy. As one of the original colonies, it was home to a diverse mix of religious minorities, and many of these remain in Pennsylvania even today, calling the rural areas of the state home. A visit to Lancaster, for example, will let you take a peek into the lifestyle of the Amish community, largely unchanged for hundreds of years. Pennsylvania really does have a little of everything!

The State Motto: "VIRTUE, LIBERTY, AND INDEPENDENCE"

The Facts: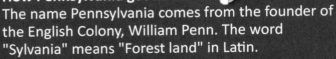
Pennsylvania became the 2nd state on December 12, 1787.
Major cities: Philadelphia, Pittsburgh, Allentown, Erie, Reading, Scranton, Bethlehem
Border states: Ohio, West Virginia, Maryland, Delaware, New Jersey, New York

How Pennsylvania got its name:
The name Pennsylvania comes from the founder of the English Colony, William Penn. The word "Sylvania" means "Forest land" in Latin.

Fun Laws: 😄
• You may not catch a fish with your hands.
• You may not catch a fish by any body part except the mouth.

Good to know!
• Pennsylvania is called the Keystone State because of its central location of the original 13 colonies.
• The first zoo in America was the Philadelphia Zoo opened in 1874, which is the oldest zoo in the country.
• The Liberty Bell, located in Philadelphia, is known as a symbol of American Independence.

The Green Animals Topiary Garden is the oldest and most northern topiary garden in the United States. It has around 20 trees, all shaped to look like animals.

State Flower:
Violet

Rhode Island designated the quahaug as the official state shell in 1987. New England tribes made valuable beads called wampum from these shells.

MASSACHUSETTS

• **Woonsocket**

Blackstone
River

Chepachet
River

Woonasquatucket
River

Pawtucket

PROVIDENCE

Jerimoth Hill
812 ft.

Scituate
Reservoir

Cranston •

Pautuxet
River

CONNECTICUT

• **Warwick**

• **Bristol**

NARRAGANSETT BAY

Prudence
Island

AQUIDNECK ISLAND

Queen
River

Wood
River

Conanicut
Island

**Little
Compton**

• **Newport**

Worden Pond

• **Narragansett**

Watchaug Pond

Pawcatuck
River

ATLANTIC
OCEAN

The first Newport Jazz Festival, known as **the First Annual American Jazz Festival**, was held in 1954. It is now world famous.

Newport is considered one of the sailing capitals of the world.

House On The Rocks. Clingstone is a house, built in 1905, situated on top of a rocky island that is only a few yards larger than the house itself!

RHODE ISLAND/RI

WELCOME TO THE OCEAN STATE

The Basics:
Total area: 1,545 sq. mi (2,678 sq. km)
Land area: 1,034 sq. mi (2,678 sq. km)
Population: 1,059,600
Capital: Providence

STORY TO KNOW

Although Rhode Island was one of the first states ever visited, by Italian explorer Giovanni Verrazzano in 1524, it did not become a state until 12 others already had before it, and even today it retains many of its indigenous place names. Rhode Island has always stood for values of fairness and freedom, making it a popular destination for industry, commerce, and immigration alike. Today, along with many of the economies of its neighbors elsewhere in the Northeastern regions of the country, Rhode Island has seen a transition to tourism and high-tech industry. Nonetheless, much of its old-world history remains in architecture, museums, and heritage sites.

Rhode Island has a coastline that is famous nationwide, and its unique attractions include baseball games with the Pawtucket Red Sox, the Beavertail Lighthouse, and Block Island. It may be America's smallest state, but it's far from the least interesting! Mansions from the heyday of the cultural elite in the 1800s are open to visitors, the first town founded by a woman in the United States, and both fresh and saltwater beaches to swim in are just a few of the places you'll be lucky enough to enjoy on a visit here!

The State Motto: "HOPE"

The Facts: 😎
Rhode Island became the 13th state on May 29, 1790.
Major cities: Providence, Warwick, Cranston, Pawtucket, East Providence
Border states: Connecticut, Massachusetts, New York (maritime border)

How Rhode Island got its name:
One source says the name came from Dutch explorer Adriaen Block, who called the land "Roodt Eylandt," which means "Red Island." He got this name from the red clay of the Rhode Island coastline.

Other sources claim that the name comes from Italian explorer Giovanni da Verrazzano, who thought one of the islands off the coast of Rhode Island looked like the island Rhodes, off the coast of Greece.

Fun Laws: 😄
• No one may bite off another's leg.

Good to know!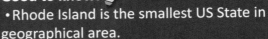
• Rhode Island is the smallest US State in geographical area.
• It was the last of the original thirteen colonies to become a state.

State Flower: Yellow Jasmine

The Peachoid is a 135 ft. tall giant water tower in Gaffney, well known for its peaches. This town is thus nicknamed the "Peach Capital of South Carolina."

In 2007, **the world's tallest sand castle** was built on Myrtle Beach and awarded with a Guinness World Record.

Sassafras Mt. 3,560 ft.

Gaffney•
Spartanburg•
•Greenville
Rock Hill•

Blue Ridge Mountains
•Lake Keowee

NORTH CAROLINA

Hartwell Lake

Saluda River

Broad River

Wateree River

Lynches River

Pee Dee River

COLUMBIA

Lake Murray

•Sumter

Myrtle Beach•

State Bird: Carolina Wren

Congaree River

Lake Marion

Santee River

South Carolina's Atlantic coastline is a popular playground for vacationers filled with pristine beaches, towering sand dunes, and dense maritime forests.

Savannah River

GEORGIA

Edisto River

Lake Moultrie

•North Charleston

Charleston•

Combahee River

Edisto Island

Hilton Head Island

ATLANTIC OCEAN

The Angel Oak Tree is thought to be one of the oldest living organisms east of the Mississippi River. It stands 65 ft. tall and the largest branch reaches 187 ft.

Pirates terrorized the Carolina coast in 1717-18.

SOUTH CAROLINA / SC

WELCOME TO THE PALMETTO STATE

The Basics:
Total area: 32,020 sq. mi (82,933 sq. km)
Land area: 30,061 sq. mi (77,857 sq. km)
Population: 5,024,400
Capital: Columbia

STORY TO KNOW

The first European settlements in South Carolina were established in modern-day Charleston. Through slave labor and production of cotton, rice, and indigo, the region prospered, eventually becoming the eighth state in 1788. It was also the first state to secede during the Civil War, with the war's first shots being fired at Fort Sumter. Post-war South Carolina struggled, as did much of the South, but today its Atlantic coast sees tourists from all over the country, and its major cities represent important stops along the highway corridors of the Eastern seaboard.

The summer time in South Carolina is just about the best the United States has to offer. Waterfalls, rivers, historic plantation sites, the Blue Ridge Mountains, and meadows filled with wildflowers will all greet visitors in the warm sunshine. The cuisine, distinctly southern, includes seafood, gumbo, and jasmine, all served with a characteristic southern charm that is unique to the region. Even though summer in Charleston doesn't last forever, the mild winters in between each high season will have you believing it never left!

The State Motto: "WHILE I BREATHE, I HOPE"

The Facts: 🤓
South Carolina became the 8th state on May 23, 1788.
Major cities: Columbia, Charleston, North Charleston, Mount Pleasant, Rock Hill
Border states: North Carolina, Georgia

How South Carolina got its name: 🤪
The Carolinas were both named in honor of King Charles I. The Latin for "Charles" is translated as "Carolus."

Fun Laws: 😄 😄
• No work may be done on Sunday.

Good to know!
• There are rumors that a water monster lurks in the depths of Lake Murray.
• Before South Carolina adopted the Palmetto State as its nickname, it was called the Iodine State.
• The first shots of the Civil War were in South Carolina at Fort Sumter.

South Dakota, a leader in honey production, designated the honeybee as its official state insect in 1978. Honeybees play an important role in agriculture.

The Sturgis Motorcycle Rally is the world's largest motorcycle rally, held annually in Sturgis, usually during the first full week of August.

Mount Rushmore symbolizes the ideals of freedom, democracy, and the American dream through its four, 60-foot granite faces. This is a mountain carving that includes Presidents George Washington, Thomas Jefferson, Theodore Roosevelt, and Abraham Lincoln.

MONTANA

NORTH DAKOTA

Lake Traverse ○

Grand River

Big Stone Lake

Moreau River

Aberdeen ●

Watertown ●

● Castle Rock
GEOGRAPHIC CENTER OF THE USA

○ Lake Oahe

PIERRE

Cheyenne River

State Bird:
Ring-necked Pheasant

BLACK HILLS

● Rapid City
🔺 Mount Rushmore 5,600 ft.
🔺 Harney Peak 7,242 ft.

Jewel Cave

White River

Huron ●

Brookings ●

James River

Big Sioux River

MN

State Flower:
American Pasque Flower

Wind Cave

● Hot Springs

Little White River

Mitchell ●

WYOMING

Wounded Knee ●

Missouri River

Sioux Falls ●

IOWA

NEBRASKA

Yankton ● Vermillion ●

The "City of Presidents" sculptures in Rapid City reveal this region's patriotism and fondness for our nation's leaders. There, you can find a bronze statue of each president.

The Badlands is one of the most unique places in America. Mystical, dramatic pinnacles rise over the prairie, leaving spectators in awe and wondering whether they are even still on Earth.

In 1892, South Dakota was begging for settlers. In order to showcase their magnificently rich soil, local officials commissioned the building of **the Corn Palace** in the middle of Mitchell, a town that today bills itself as the **"Corn Capital of the World."**

SOUTH DAKOTA/SD

WELCOME TO THE MOUNT RUSHMORE STATE

The Basics:
Total area: 77,116 sq. mi (199,729 sq. km)
Land area: 75,811 sq. mi (196,350 sq. km)
Population: 869,665
Capital: Pierre

STORY TO KNOW

Recognized around the world for its most famous monument, Mount Rushmore, South Dakota was the 40th state along with its northern neighbor. After a discovery of gold in the region in 1879, the Native Americans who called this land home, the Lakota, were quickly routed, though they fought long and hard to retain what land they could. Today, nearly 9 percent of South Dakota's people are indigenous, with numerous reservations across the region. With pine-covered hills and vast prairies, it's easy to see why the land was so highly coveted.

The Black Hills of South Dakota are so-named for the dark, coniferous trees that dot the hills of the state. The wilderness here represents nearly every part of the Midwest, and many travelers who seek solitary enjoyment of nature come here for that very reason. Gold mines, archaeological digs, dinosaur fossils, and much more can all be found here. In fact, the most complete Tyrannosaurus Rex skeleton ever uncovered, ironically named Sue, was uncovered in South Dakota! Visit for Mount Rushmore and Crazy Horse Memorial, to be sure – these monuments are truly a marvel to behold – but stay for the real beauty of the state, to be found in every corner of its pristine landscapes.

The State Motto: "UNDER GOD, THE PEOPLE RULE"

The Facts: 😎
South Dakota became the 40th state on November 2, 1889.
Major cities: Sioux Falls, Rapid City, Aberdeen, Brookings, Watertown
Border states: Nebraska, Iowa, Minnesota, North Dakota, Montana, Wyoming

How South Dakota got its name: 🤪
The name Dakota comes from the Sioux Indian word for "Friend" or "Ally."

Fun Laws: 😄
• No horses are allowed into Fountain Inn unless they are wearing pants.

Good to know! 💡
• Harney Peak is the highest US mountain east of the Rockies.
• Each head-on Mount Rushmore is 60 ft. tall!
• North Dakota and South Dakota were admitted on the same day to avoid a feud between the states.

Reelfoot Lake, a shallow lake, was formed by the earthquakes in the winter of 1811–12. In the upheaval, land on the east side of the Mississippi River sank, creating a depression that river water rushed in to fill. The lake has a surface area of some 23 sq. mi. but an average depth of only about 5 ft.

The Minister's Treehouse is the world's largest treehouse. Located just outside of Crossville, Tennessee, the 97-foot-tall tree house and church is supported by a still-living 80-foot-tall white oak tree with a 12-foot diameter base, relying on six other oaks for support.

The Sunsphere Tower. Built for the 1982 World's Fair, this iconic tower symbolizes the fair's theme: "Energy Turns the World."

KENTUCKY

Cumberland River

CUMBERLAND MTS.

VIRGINIA

MISSOURI

Mississippi River

Tennessee River

APPALACHIAN MTS.

NASHVILLE

Oak Ridge

Knoxville

NC

ARKANSAS

CUMBERLAND PLATEAU

Clingmans Dome 6.643 ft.

•**Memphis**

Shelbyville

Tennessee River

Dollywood
Love every moment

MS

ALABAMA

GA

Chattanooga

State Bird: Mockingbird

Dollywood is a theme park. In addition to standard amusement park thrill rides, Dollywood features traditional crafts and music from the Smoky Mountain area. The park hosts a number of concerts and musical events annually.

State Flower: Iris

Ripley's Aquarium is currently the top-rated aquarium in the United States. The aquarium's 1.4 million gallons of water are home to over 100,000 exotic sea creatures.

Great Smoky Mountains National Park is the most-visited national park in the United States. The park encompasses 816.28 sq. mi., making it one of the largest protected areas in the eastern United States. Also, this park is known as the "Salamander Capital of The World."

TENNESSEE / TN

WELCOME TO THE VOLUNTEER STATE

The Basics:
Total area: 42,144 sq. mi (109,153 sq. km)
Land area: 41,235 sq. mi (106,798 sq. km)
Population: 6,716,000
Capital: Nashville

STORY TO KNOW

There's nowhere in the world like Tennessee. Nashville, the "Music City," is home to the biggest country and western stars in the world, and Memphis as well is arguably the birthplace of the blues. With ten state songs (more than any other state), it's easy to see why so much music comes from this one place. The Opry hosts the America's longest-running radio show to boot, and Memphis' 70-foot-long guitar building is a tourist spectacle you won't want to miss.

The state of Tennessee was the 16th state in America, and beyond its musical roots, it also has industries in hydro power, tourism, and water management. With several national parks, the great Smoky Mountains, and camping like you won't find anywhere else, there's plenty of reasons for Tennessee to top people's lists for their next vacation. It's also one of the best places to live in the South, consistently ranking higher in quality of life than many of its counterparts south of the Mason-Dixon line.

The State Motto: "AGRICULTURE AND COMMERCE"

The Facts: 🤓
Tennessee became the 16th state on June 1, 1796.
Major cities: Memphis, Nashville, Knoxville, Chattanooga, Clarksville
Border states: Kentucky, Virginia, North Carolina, Georgia, Alabama, Mississippi, Arkansas, Missouri

How Tennessee got its name: 😜
Tennessee comes from the name of a Cherokee Indian village called "Tanasi."

Fun Laws: 😂
• It is a crime to share your Netflix password in Tennessee.

Good to know!
• From Lookout Mountain, you can see parts of 7 different states.
• The world's largest freshwater aquarium is in Chattanooga.
• It is called the Volunteer State because when soldiers were needed in the War of 1812, Tennessee soldiers volunteered and helped to defeat the British at the Battle of Orleans.

Waco Mammoth National Monument is a paleontological site protecting the remains of 24 mammoths from the Ice Age. The national park features fossils of female mammoths, a bull mammoth, and an ancient relative of camels, as well as an antelope, alligator, giant tortoise, and more.

The Congress Avenue Bridge. This bridge is currently home to the world's largest urban bat colony, containing about 1.5 million bats.

State Flower:
Bluebonnet

OK

Canadian River

NEW MEXICO

•Amarillo

Wichita Falls•

•Lubbock

Red River

Texarkana•

ARKANSAS

Fort Worth• •Dallas

•Abilene

Brazos River

Neches River

•El Paso

Guadalupe Peak 8,751 ft.

Pecos River

CHISOS MOUNTAINS

Colorado River

•Waco

Trinity River

MEXICO

Rio Grande

AUSTIN

San Antonio•

•Houston

Guadalupe River

Nueces River

GULF OF MEXICO

The Houston Livestock Show and Rodeo, also called Rodeo Houston, is the largest livestock exhibition and rodeo in the world.

Texas leads all states in the production of oil.

Space Center Houston is one of the only places on Earth where visitors can see astronauts train for missions, touch a real moon rock, and take a behind-the-scenes tour of NASA.

The Battle of the Alamo was a pivotal event in the Texas Revolution. In 1836, there was a 13-day siege at a mission in San Antonio. The battle was between Mexican forces of about 4000, under President General Santa Anna, against a handful of 180 American rebels fighting for Texan independence from Mexico.

State Bird:
Mockingbird

TEXAS TX

WELCOME TO THE LONE STAR STATE

The Basics:
Total area: 268,596 sq. mi (695,662 sq. km)
Land area: 261,232 sq. mi (676,587 sq. km)
Population: 28,304,600
Capital: Austin

STORY TO KNOW

The Lone Star state is perhaps the most well-known and most-often characterized region in America. It's the largest state in the contiguous United States, and as they say, everything really is bigger there. Its size, geographic diversity, natural resources, and fiercely independent history all combine to make Texas practically its own country. The battle-cry of "Remember the Alamo!" has still not been forgotten here. Today, it leads the nation in oil production, beef production, and has the largest capital building in America. Its people, while proud and no-nonsense, are also well-known for their generosity and compassion.

Texas is home to a stunning diversity of landscapes: from hill country painted with wildflowers to swamps and islands along the Gulf Coast, and from sandy desert plains in West Texas to the Rio Grande, separating the state from Mexico, there is plenty of raw, natural beauty on display. You can go rafting, caving, hiking, camping, swimming, and much, much more here! Or, if you prefer, you can instead spend time in any of its world-class cities. Houston, Austin, and Dallas are just the three largest – the state has plenty of other towns and cities full of life and friendly folks who would be happy to barbecue up some delicious Texas beef with you.

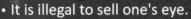

The State Motto: "FRIENDSHIP"

The Facts: 🤓
Texas became the 28th state on December 29, 1845.
Major cities: Houston, San Antonio, Dallas, Austin, Fort Worth, El Paso
Border states: New Mexico, Oklahoma, Arkansas, Louisiana

How Texas got its name: 😜
The name Texas comes from the Caddo Native American word "Tejas", which means "Friends."

Fun Laws: 😄
• It is illegal to sell one's eye.
• It is illegal to milk another person's cow.

Good to know!
• Texas has been a member of six different nations including Spain, Mexico, France, the Republic of Texas, the Confederate States, and the USA.
• Dr. Pepper was invented in Waco, TX.
• The King Ranch in Texas is bigger than the state of Rhode Island.

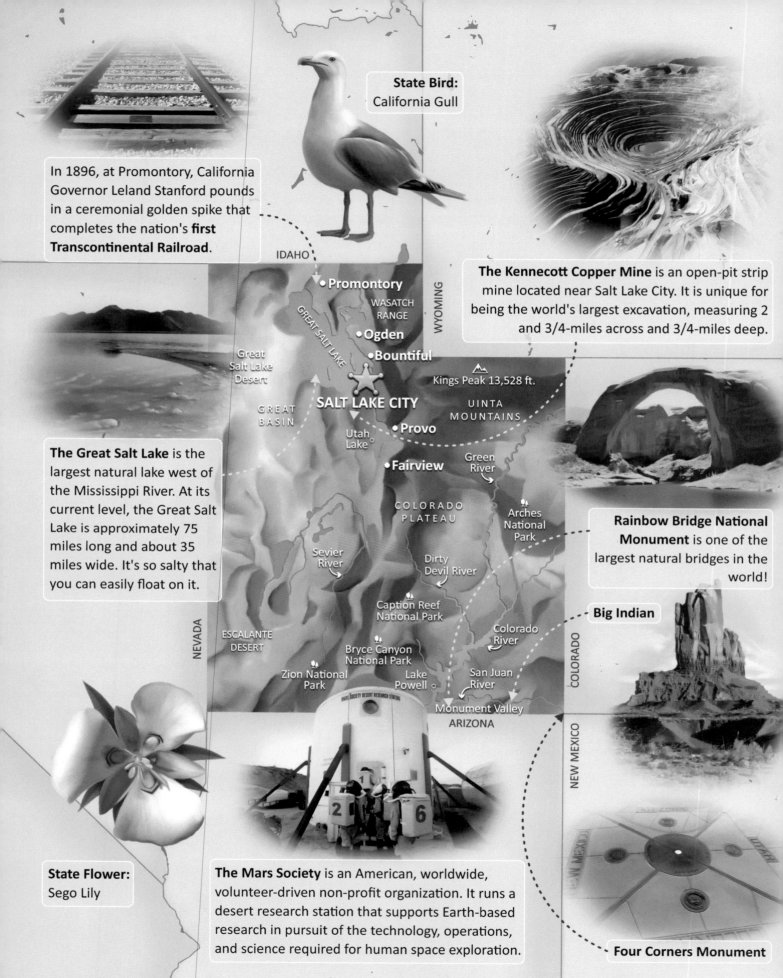

State Bird:
California Gull

In 1896, at Promontory, California Governor Leland Stanford pounds in a ceremonial golden spike that completes the nation's **first Transcontinental Railroad**.

The Kennecott Copper Mine is an open-pit strip mine located near Salt Lake City. It is unique for being the world's largest excavation, measuring 2 and 3/4-miles across and 3/4-miles deep.

The Great Salt Lake is the largest natural lake west of the Mississippi River. At its current level, the Great Salt Lake is approximately 75 miles long and about 35 miles wide. It's so salty that you can easily float on it.

Rainbow Bridge National Monument is one of the largest natural bridges in the world!

IDAHO

- **Promontory**

WASATCH RANGE

- **Ogden**
- **Bountiful**

WYOMING

GREAT SALT LAKE

Great Salt Lake Desert

Kings Peak 13,528 ft.

⭐ **SALT LAKE CITY**

GREAT BASIN

UINTA MOUNTAINS

- **Provo**

Utah Lake

- **Fairview**

Green River

COLORADO PLATEAU

Arches National Park

Sevier River

Dirty Devil River

NEVADA

ESCALANTE DESERT

Caption Reef National Park

Colorado River

Bryce Canyon National Park

Zion National Park

Lake Powell

San Juan River

COLORADO

Big Indian

Monument Valley

ARIZONA

NEW MEXICO

State Flower:
Sego Lily

The Mars Society is an American, worldwide, volunteer-driven non-profit organization. It runs a desert research station that supports Earth-based research in pursuit of the technology, operations, and science required for human space exploration.

Four Corners Monument

UTAH / UT

WELCOME TO THE BEEHIVE STATE

The Basics:
Total area: 84,897 sq. mi (219,882 sq. km)
Land area: 82,170 sq. mi (212,818 sq. km)
Population: 3,101,800
Capital: Salt Lake City

STORY TO KNOW

Utah, home of mountains, desert, canyons, rivers, and more, is named after the Ute, a hunter-gatherer group of Native Americans who populated a region of the state long before it was ever colonized by Europeans. The Spanish in the late 1700s and trappers through the early to mid-1800s were the first of these, but it wasn't until 1847, when the Mormons arrived seeking a refuge in which to practice their religion, that large-scale settlement would begin. In the 1860s, the discovery of precious metals led to further expansion and settlement of the state.

Today, Salt Lake City is the headquarters of the Church of Latter-day Saints (the Mormon Church), and they have shaped the political landscape of Utah for over a century. Stunning natural beauty is abundant here, and in the surround regions of the state as well, with over 65% of it set aside either as National Park or as areas for the defense industries and military testing. From Arches to Zion, many believe there is no greater beauty than what you will find here. Its rainbow-colored canyons and windswept plateaus are a mecca for hikers, climbers, campers, and photographers from around the world.

The State Motto: "INDUSTRY"

The Facts:
Utah became the 45th state on January 4, 1896.
Major cities: Salt Lake City, West Valley City, Provo, West Jordan, Orem
Border states: Idaho, Wyoming, Colorado, Arizona, Nevada, New Mexico

How Utah got its name:
The name Utah comes from the Ute Indians and means "People of the mountains."

Fun Laws:
• It is against the law to fish from horseback.
• It is illegal **not to** drink milk.

Good to know!
• The Great Salt Lake is the largest lake west of the Mississippi River.
• Utah is one of the Four Corners states. It meets up with Colorado, Arizona, and New Mexico at a single point.
• Utah has the highest literacy rate of any state in the US.

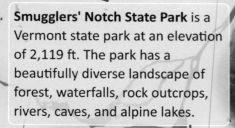

Smugglers' Notch State Park is a Vermont state park at an elevation of 2,119 ft. The park has a beautifully diverse landscape of forest, waterfalls, rock outcrops, rivers, caves, and alpine lakes.

State Flower: Red Clover

The sugar maple was designated the state tree of Vermont in 1949. Trees are tapped in late winter to get maple sap.

Town Meeting Day. On Town Meeting Day, the first Tuesday in March, citizens across Vermont come together in their communities to discuss the business of their towns.

CANADA

Lake Champlain

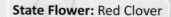

• Burlington

Mt. Mansfield 4,393 ft.

St. Johnsbury

Winooski River

MONTPELIER

• Barre

• Middlebury

Connecticut River

Otter Creek

GREEN MOUNTAINS

White River

NEW HAMPSHIRE

Woodstock

• Rutland

NEW YORK

Springfield •

Vermont has three official state rocks – **marble, granite, and slate**. These three types of rocks are found in the ground in different places throughout the state. This rock from Vermont has been used for buildings and monuments all over the country.

• Bennington

Brattleboro •

MASSACHUSETTS

The Bennington Battle Monument is 306 ft., 4 and 1/2 inches tall and was completed and dedicated in 1891. The Monument was built to commemorate the Battle of Bennington, which occurred on August 16, 1777, and is considered to be the turning point in the Revolutionary War.

State Bird: Hermit Thrush

A lot of electronics and electrical parts are made in Vermont.

VERMONT/VT

WELCOME TO THE GREEN MOUNTAIN STATE

The Basics:
Total area: 9,616 sq. mi (24,906 sq. km)
Land area: 9,217 sq. mi (23,871 sq. km)
Population: 623,657
Capital: Montpelier

STORY TO KNOW

Vermont is a small, quiet state in the northeastern United States. It was the 14th to enter the union, and it was actually a region of considerable conflict between the French and English well into the late 1700s, until the people of the state declared their independence in 1777. Vermont is layered in lush forest and has many caves and mountains to explore. It's also famous for its maple syrup and its winter skiing. The name Vermont comes from the French phrase for "Green Mountain," referring to the treed hills throughout the state.

Vermont may be small, but it is home to both the world's largest deep hole granite quarry and underground marble quarry. These bolster its main industries of forestry, pulp, and furniture, all owing to the nearly 50 species of trees that grow in abundance throughout the state. Tourism also sees many people from around the country and the world visiting Vermont, whether it's to take in a ski season in the winter time or explore the verdant forests in the summer. No matter the time of year, though, the maple syrup is always flowing!

The State Motto: "FREEDOM AND UNITY"

The Facts: 🤓
Vermont became the 14th state on March 4, 1791.
Major cities: Burlington, Essex, South Burlington, Colchester, Rutland
Border states: New Hampshire, New York, Massachusetts

How Vermont got its name: 🤪
Vermont is derived from two French words, "Mont" and "Vert," meaning "Green mountain." The name was suggested by Dr. Thomas Young in 1777.

Fun Laws: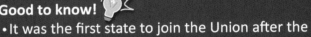
• It is illegal to deny the existence of God.

Good to know! 💡
• It was the first state to join the Union after the original 13 colonies.
• It is the second smallest state by population (after Wyoming).
• It was one of the first states to outlaw slavery.

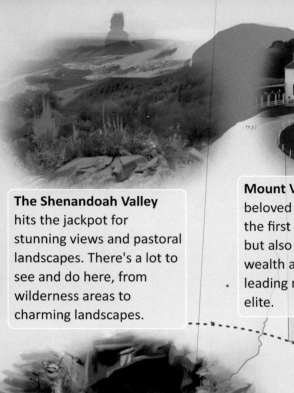

The Shenandoah Valley hits the jackpot for stunning views and pastoral landscapes. There's a lot to see and do here, from wilderness areas to charming landscapes.

Mount Vernon was not only the beloved home of George Washington, the first president of the United States, but also the source of much of his wealth and the mark of his status as a leading member of the Virginia planter elite.

The 23-mile Chesapeake Bay Bridge is a dual-span bridge in Virginia. It connects the state's rural Eastern Shore region with the urban Western Shore.

The Natural Bridge is 215 ft. of solid rock, carved by the fingers of nature. For years, water carved away at the soft rock, eventually leaving this bridge in its wake.

MARYLAND

WEST VIRGINIA

SHENANDOAH VALLEY

Arlington•

Mt. Vernon•

Rappahannock River

Potomac River

State Flower: Flowering Dogwood

•**Charlottesville**

James River

BLUE RIDGE MOUNTAINS

•**Lexington**

KENTUCKY

★ RICHMOND

Jamestown

CHESAPEAKE BAY

•**Roanoke**

Roanoke River

Newport News•

Norfolk•

Mt. Rogers 5,729 ft.

TENNESSEE

NORTH CAROLINA

The Cumberland Gap is nature's passage through the Cumberland Mountains between Kentucky, Tennessee, and Virginia. Native Americans and early pioneers used it as a footpath through the mountains.

State Bird: Cardinal

The Norfolk Naval Base is the world's largest naval station, supporting 75 ships and 134 aircraft alongside 14 piers and 11 aircraft hangars.

VIRGINIA / VA

WELCOME TO THE OLD DOMINION STATE

The Basics:
Total area: 42,775 sq. mi (110,787 sq. km)
Land area: 39,490 sq. mi (102,279 sq. km)
Population: 8,470,000
Capital: Richmond

STORY TO KNOW

Virginia is among the most historic states in the nation. Four of the first five US presidents hailed from here, and the very first permanent English colony in the New World was established in Virginia in 1607: Jamestown, a merchant town that grew into a prosperous colony. With tobacco plantations and slave labor, Virginia grew into one of the most important of the original thirteen colonies, and the final battle of the Revolutionary War was fought here, at Yorktown. While its countryside and economy were devastated after secession and defeat in the Civil War, modern-day Virginia has recovered well and boasts high-tech industry as well as government work.

Situated across the Potomac from Washington D.C., the "Birthplace of America" sees large shipbuilding contracts, US naval presence, rolling green hills, Atlantic shoreline, and numerous historical sites all in the same small state. Its key role in the early days of America and its lasting presence in American political life have made Virginia a place that punches well above its weight, and even pre-Revolution, King Charles I of England fondly referred to Virginians as "the best of his distant children." One visit to these iconic shores, and you'll understand why!

The State Motto: "THUS ALWAYS TO TYRANTS"

The Facts: 🤓
Virginia became the 10th state on June 25, 1788.
Major cities: Virginia Beach, Norfolk, Chesapeake, Richmond, Newport News, Alexandria
Border states: North Carolina, Tennessee, Kentucky, West Virginia, Maryland, Washington D.C.

How Virginia got its name: 🤓
The name Virginia comes from Queen Elizabeth I, who was known as the Virgin Queen.

Fun Laws: 😄
• Children are not to go trick-or-treating on Halloween.
• It is illegal to tickle women.

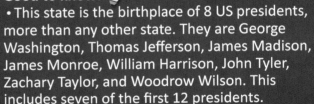

Good to know!
• This state is the birthplace of 8 US presidents, more than any other state. They are George Washington, Thomas Jefferson, James Madison, James Monroe, William Harrison, John Tyler, Zachary Taylor, and Woodrow Wilson. This includes seven of the first 12 presidents.
• Richmond was capital of the Confederate States during the Civil War.
• You can visit both George Washington's home (Mount Vernon) and Thomas Jefferson's home (Monticello) in Virginia.

Olympic National Park holds the largest number of Roosevelt elk living anywhere (about 5,000). This subspecies is the state mammal of Washington.

The World's Tallest Totem Pole is in Tacoma. It's 105 ft. high and was carved in Tacoma from a single cedar by Indian sculptors brought to the state from Alaska.

Microsoft Corporation is headquartered in Redmond, WA. Bill Gates, the head of Microsoft and the one of richest men in the world, also lives in this state.

CANADA

Pend Oreille River

San Juan Island

• Bellingham

Strait of Juan de Fuca

Skagit River

Okanogan River

ROCKY MOUNTAINS

CASCADE MOUNTAINS

Puget Sound

Lake Chelan

Spokane River

OLYMPIC MOUNTAINS

Redmond•

Wenatchee River

Grand Coulee Dam

• Seattle

Spokane•

• Tacoma

Wenatchee•

COLUMBIA PLATEAU

OLYMPIA

Columbia River

IDAHO

• Centralia

Mt. Rainier 14,410 ft.

Yakima•

Yakima River

Snake River

Mt. St. Helens erupted

• Vancouver

Columbia River

• Walla Walla

OREGON

PACIFIC OCEAN

State Flower: Pacific rhododendron

The Space Needle is an observation tower in Seattle, which provides a 360° view of the city. Its peak, an aircraft warning beacon, reaches 605 ft.

Washington produces about 70% of the apples grown in the United States.

STARBUCKS COFFEE · TEA · SPICES

In 1971, **Starbucks** opened its first store in Seattle. The name, inspired by Moby Dick, evoked the romance of the high seas and the seafaring tradition of the early coffee traders.

State Bird: Goldfinch

WASHINGTON/WA

WELCOME TO THE EVERGREEN STATE

The Basics:
Total area: 71,298 sq. mi (184,661 sq. km)
Land area: 66,456 sq. mi (172,119 sq. km)
Population: 7,405,700
Capital: Olympia

STORY TO KNOW

North of Oregon on the Pacific Northwest is Washington, the only state named after a president! Abundant in seafood, natural beauty, running fresh water, and lush evergreen forest, it's not hard to see why the state is so widely admired and boasted about by its residents. Adventurers and photographers from around the world flock here to capture its beauty and enjoy its mild climate. Seattle, the state's largest city, is also a major North American seaport, with a diverse economy and a massive shipping industry. Tech giants like Microsoft and Amazon call this city home and provide thousands of jobs to its residents.

Washington is also the largest producer of organic apples in the world, and it grows other fruits like cherries and raspberries as well. Starbucks was founded here, and it is home to the longest floating bridge in the world. With such a diverse range of industries, natural sights, interesting activities, and generous people on offer, Washington truly provides one of the best experiences for its residents and visitors alike that America can provide!

The State Motto: "BY AND BY"

The Facts:
Washington became the 42nd state on November 11, 1889.
Major cities: Seattle, Spokane, Tacoma, Vancouver, Bellevue, Kent
Border states: Oregon, Idaho

How Washington got its name:
The state is named after the first president of the United States, George Washington.

Fun Laws:
• No person may walk about in public if he or she has the common cold.
• All lollipops are banned.

Good to know!
• It is the only state to be named for a US president. The residents had recommended Columbia, but Congress decided to name the land after George Washington.

The Pentagon, located just outside Washington, D.C., in Virginia, is the headquarters of the U.S. Department of Defense, located in a massive, five-sided concrete and steel building that serves as a potent symbol of America's military strength.

The Vietnam Veterans Memorial Wall. This memorial honors members of the U.S. armed forces who fought, died in service, or were listed MIA during the Vietnam War. The number of names on the wall totals 58,220.

The National Air and Space Museum maintains the largest collection of historic air and spacecraft in the world. It was established in 1946 and now it is the third most-visited museum in the world and the most-visited museum in the United States!

The Library of Congress is the largest library in the world! It houses more than 164 million items, from books to photos to recordings to maps to much, much more.

District of Columbia

White House

Pennsylvania Ave.

The Ellipse

The Lincoln Memorial

Tidal Basin

Supreme Count

Library of Congress

Smithsonian Institution

District Bird: Wood Thrush

The Lincoln Memorial is a tribute to President Abraham Lincoln, who fought to preserve the nation during the Civil War, from 1861-1865. The structure's 36 columns represent the 36 states in the Union at the time of Lincoln's death.

Potomac River

District Flower: American Beauty Rose

The Washington Monument dominates the United States Capitol skyline as a symbolic tribute to George Washington's military leadership, humble statesmanship, and Presidential fortitude and wisdom. Constructed from marble, granite, and gneiss, the monument is the world's tallest free-standing stone structure, towering more than 555 ft. high.

Since 1800, **The White House** has been a symbol of the United States government, the president, and the people of America. It has also served as the home of every U.S. president except George Washington.

WASHINGTON D.C.

WELCOME TO THE DISTRICT

The Basics:
Statehood: June 11, 1800
Total area: 68,34 sq. mi (177,0 sq. km)
Land area: 61,05 sq. mi (158,1 sq. km)
Population: 703,608
Capital: The Capital of the U.S.

STORY TO KNOW

Not quite a state, but more than a city, Washington D.C. is the proud capital city of the entire United States. The location was chosen as a compromise between the North and the South (Maryland and Virginia), and the land ceded for the city does not officially belong to any one state. As the seat of the entire US government, it represents the history and longstanding political traditions of the country. George Washington himself appointed an architect, Pierre L'Enfant, to design the city, and this design is still visible today.

Sitting along the banks of the iconic Potomac River, Washington D.C. is home to many monuments, including Capitol Hill, the White House, the Martin Luther King Jr. Memorial, and the Supreme Court Building. The world-famous Smithsonian museum is also here, with free entry for any and all! Although many of its residents have been pushing for statehood, whether Washington D.C. ever becomes the 51st state or not, it is still an amazing and historic city to visit – or perhaps even to move to!

The District Motto: "JUSTICE FOR ALL"

How Washington D.C. got its name: 😎
The official name of the city is District of Columbia. The Washington is for George Washington and the C (Columbia) is for Christopher Columbus.

Good to know!
• Not a state, this area is both the city of Washington (the capital of the United States) and the District of Columbia.
• The flag of D.C. was based off of George Washington's family's coat of arms.
• The states of Maryland and Virginia ceded land for Washington D.C.
• George Washington never got to live in the White House. It wasn't officially called the White House until 1901. Before that it was referred to as the President's House or Palace.

99

Marble King. West Virginia is a world center of glass marble manufacturing. Did you know that over one million marbles a day are produced by a West Virginia company?

The nation's first Mother's Day was held at a local Church in Grafton, WV. Anna Jarvis organized the holiday in 1908 in memory of her mother.

The Mothman is the West Virginia legend that become so well-known due to the self-titled book and movie. This urban cryptid legend even has his own massive statue.

State Bird: Northern Cardinal

Weirton

Wheeling

PENNSYLVANIA

OHIO

Ohio River

Morgantown

Fairmont

Grafton

Cheat River

Tygart Lake

Parkersburg

MARYLAND

Potomac River

Harpers Ferry

Shenandoah River

ALLEGHENY MOUNTAINS

APPALACHIAN MOUNTAINS

Tygart Valley River

CHEAT MOUNTAINS

△ Spruce Knob 4,863 ft.

Greenbank

Sutton Lake

Elk River

VIRGINIA

Kanawha River

Summerville Lake

CHARLESTON

Huntington

Greenbrier River

New River

Guyandotte River

Big Bend Tunnel

Tug Fork River

Beckley

Lewisburg

KENTUCKY

Bluestone River

Dedicated in 2000, **the Green Bank Telescope** is the most technically advanced single-dish radio telescope in the world. Its 110-meter by 100-meter dish boasts more than two acres of area for collecting incredibly faint radio waves from the distant universe.

Acoustic music is very popular in West Virginia. A lot of people here still make their own instruments.

Sandstone Falls is the largest waterfall on the New River, spanning 1500 feet across. Divided by islands, the falls drop from 10 to 25 ft.

State Flower: Rhododendron

WEST VIRGINIA/WV

WELCOME TO THE MOUNTAIN STATE

The Basics:
Total area: 24,230 sq. mi (62,756 sq. km)
Land area: 24,038 sq. mi (62,259 sq. km)
Population: 1,815,900
Capital: Charleston

STORY TO KNOW

Not to be confused with its neighbors, West Virginia split from Virginia during the Civil War and did not secede. It remained part of the Union primarily because its region did not depend on slave labor, and it thus became the 35th state in 1863, just as the war broke out. The region was largely inhabited by Germans, Scots, and Irish, and as the centuries past, its industries solidified themselves: coal and steel. While these resources provided much prosperity to the state at large, their mining and milling soon became synonymous with disease, poverty, and environmental devastation.

Nonetheless, West Virginia still to this day boasts some of the most iconic and rugged natural beauty that America has to offer. Their government has worked tirelessly to promote their tourism industry, and today, it has paid off. Mountains and spruce forest are the pride of this small state, and it's no wonder so much music has been inspired by this beautiful scenery. John Denver's famous "Country Roads Take Me Home" references West Virginia directly, and many citizens of the state have taken to calling their beloved region "Almost Heaven" as Denver does in the iconic tune.

The State Motto: "MOUNTAINEERS ARE ALWAYS FREE"

The Facts: 🤓
West Virginia became the 35th state on June 20, 1863.
Major cities: Charleston, Huntington, Parkersburg, Morgantown, Wheeling
Border states: Virginia, Kentucky, Ohio, Pennsylvania, Maryland

How West Virginia got its name: 😃
The name "Virginia" comes from Queen Elizabeth I, who was called the Virgin Queen. The state took the name West Virginia when it split from the state of Virginia during the Civil War.

Fun Laws: 😄 😄
• Whistling underwater is prohibited.
• For each act of public swearing a person shall be fined one dollar.

Good to know! 💡
• Some people say West Virginia is the northernmost southern state, others say it's the southernmost northern state.
• West Virginia split from Virginia during the Civil War. West Virginia wanted to stay in the Union, while Virginia wanted to become part of the Confederacy.
• Much of West Virginia is mountains, hence the name the Mountain State. Much of the state, 75%, is also covered in forest.

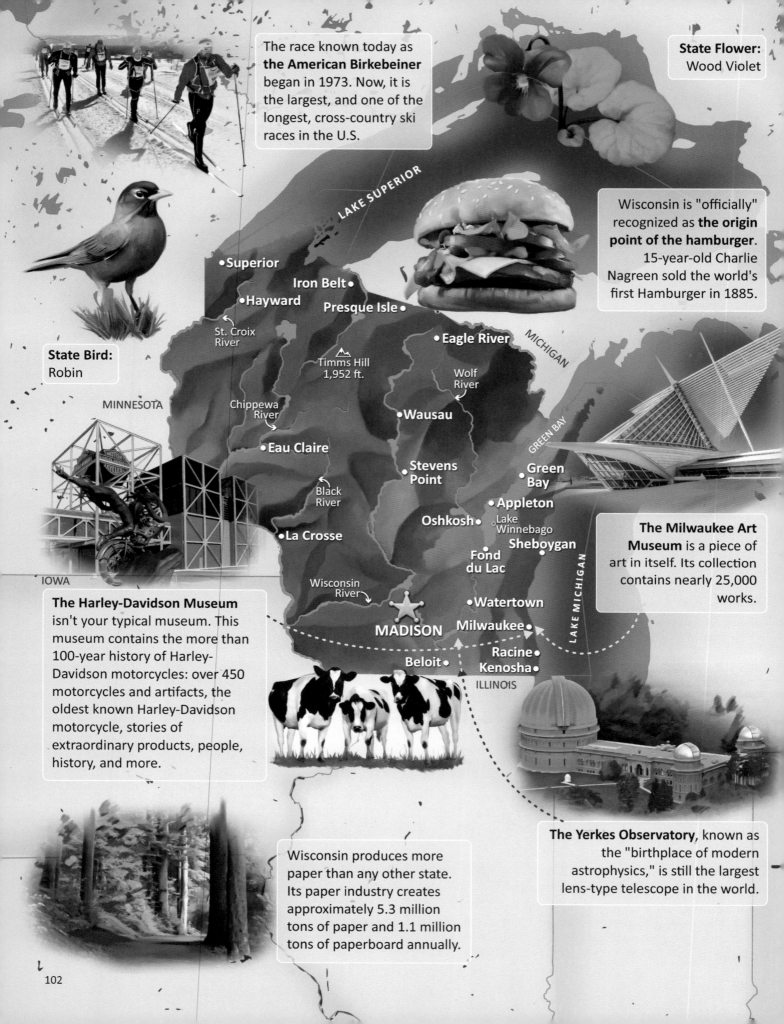

The race known today as **the American Birkebeiner** began in 1973. Now, it is the largest, and one of the longest, cross-country ski races in the U.S.

State Flower:
Wood Violet

Wisconsin is "officially" recognized as **the origin point of the hamburger**. 15-year-old Charlie Nagreen sold the world's first Hamburger in 1885.

State Bird:
Robin

LAKE SUPERIOR

•Superior

Iron Belt•

•Hayward

Presque Isle •

St. Croix River

•Eagle River

MICHIGAN

Timms Hill
1,952 ft.

Wolf River

MINNESOTA

Chippewa River

•Wausau

•Eau Claire

GREEN BAY

•Stevens Point

•Green Bay

Black River

•Appleton

Oshkosh•

•La Crosse

Lake Winnebago

Sheboygan•

IOWA

Fond du Lac

The Harley-Davidson Museum isn't your typical museum. This museum contains the more than 100-year history of Harley-Davidson motorcycles: over 450 motorcycles and artifacts, the oldest known Harley-Davidson motorcycle, stories of extraordinary products, people, history, and more.

Wisconsin River

•Watertown

★ **MADISON**

Milwaukee•

Beloit•

Racine•
Kenosha•

ILLINOIS

LAKE MICHIGAN

The Milwaukee Art Museum is a piece of art in itself. Its collection contains nearly 25,000 works.

Wisconsin produces more paper than any other state. Its paper industry creates approximately 5.3 million tons of paper and 1.1 million tons of paperboard annually.

The Yerkes Observatory, known as the "birthplace of modern astrophysics," is still the largest lens-type telescope in the world.

WISCONSIN WI

WELCOME TO THE BADGER STATE

The Basics:
Total area: 65,496 sq. mi (169,635 sq. km)
Land area: 54,158 sq. mi (140,268 sq. km)
Population: 5,795,500
Capital: Madison

STORY TO KNOW

Wisconsin is probably best-known for its dairy production – often called America's Dairyland, the state leads the nation in cheese, milk, and butter production, with over 2.8 billion pounds of cheddar, provolone, gouda, and other delicious styles of cheese being made every year! This is thanks to the more than one million cows that graze throughout Wisconsin, with farmers also growing crops like corn, soybeans, potatoes, and cranberries. Breweries and meatpacking plants in Milwaukee provide many good jobs to the city's residents, and health care, manufacturing, and paper processing and paper products shore up the state's economy even further.

Wisconsin is sparsely populated in the North, where rugged forest hills sprawl across the landscape. The state is also home to over 15,000 lakes – making it a great location for kayakers, canoers, and outdoor adventurers of all kinds. There are islands to explore along the Apostle Island National Lakeshore, and caves in Lake Superior. And while the forests provide much industry to the state by way of paper and paper products, they are still largely untouched in many areas and worth exploring on a camping trip. Finally, in the winter time, join the thousands of skiers from around the world on the American Birkebeiner – the longest cross-country ski race in the country!

The State Motto: "FORWARD"

The Facts: 😎
Wisconsin became the 30th state on May 29, 1848.
Major cities: Milwaukee, Madison, Green Bay, Kenosha, Racine
Border states: Illinois, Iowa, Minnesota, Michigan

How Wisconsin got its name: 😋
The name "Wisconsin" comes from a Native American word. It likely came from a Miami Indian word for the Wisconsin River meaning "Gathering of waters."

Fun Laws: 😂
• State Law made it illegal to serve apple pie in public restaurants without cheese.

Good to know! 💡
• The first house in the US to be wired for electricity was in Appleton, Wisconsin.
• Summerfest, held in Milwaukee, is one of the world's largest outdoor music festivals.
• The state is known for its cow farms, milk, and cheese. Fans of the Green Bay Packers football team are sometimes called cheeseheads!

The Old Faithful Geyser in Yellowstone National Park erupts every 92 minutes, around 16 times a day. This geyser spews a giant stream of water straight into the air, reaching heights of 130 to 190 ft.

Yellowstone National Park is the world's first national park. It was established on March 1, 1872. Yellowstone is larger than Rhode Island and Delaware combined.

The Wyoming Dinosaur Center is a 12,000 sq. ft. exhibition area which has over 30 mounted skeletons, a preparation lab with visitor viewing, and hundreds of displays and dioramas. There, you can also see dinosaurs buried in the ground.

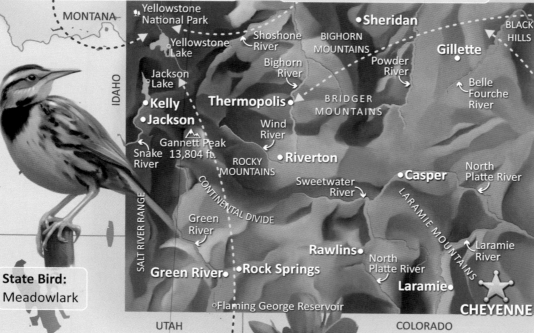

MONTANA

Yellowstone National Park
Yellowstone Lake
Shoshone River
Bighorn River
BIGHORN MOUNTAINS
•Sheridan
BLACK HILLS
Powder River
•Gillette
Belle Fourche River

IDAHO

Jackson Lake
•Kelly
•Jackson
Thermopolis•
BRIDGER MOUNTAINS
SOUTH DAKOTA

Wind River
Gannett Peak 13,804 ft.
Snake River
ROCKY MOUNTAINS
•Riverton
•Casper
North Platte River

CONTINENTAL DIVIDE
Sweetwater River
LARAMIE MOUNTAINS
NEBRASKA

SALT RIVER RANGE
Green River
Rawlins•
North Platte River
Laramie River

Green River•
•Rock Springs
Laramie•
CHEYENNE

Flaming George Reservoir

UTAH

COLORADO

State Bird: Meadowlark

State Flower: Indian Paintbrush

Devils Tower National Monument, a unique and striking geological wonder steeped in Indian legend, is a modern day national park and climbers' challenge. The Tower is a granite formation rising over 1,200 ft. into the air.

Grand Teton National Park is one of the most spectacular, awe-inspiring places in the U.S. Many peaks exceed 12,000 ft., and the highest one tops out at 13,770 ft.

There are a lot of Elks in Wyoming.

WYOMING/WY

WELCOME TO THE COWBOY STATE

The Basics:
Total area: 97,813 sq. mi (253,335 sq. km)
Land area: 97,093 sq. mi (251,470 sq. km)
Population: 579,315
Capital: Cheyenne

STORY TO KNOW

The plains and mountains of Montana were home to many of the now most-famous Native American tribes in the New World. The Lakota and Cheyenne warriors soundly defeated the American Lt. Col. George Custer in the infamous Battle of Little Bighorn. This battle was part of the larger Sioux War, which had been precipitated when gold and silver discoveries attracted many new settlers to Montana in the mid-19th century. Today, Native Americans still make up 6 percent of the state's population, though the Sioux War was eventually won by the American settlers.

Today, Montana is known for its rugged beauty — it's home to Glacier National Park and parts of Yellowstone National Park, which it shares with Idaho and Wyoming. These parks, and the splendor of the rest of the state, make Montana one of the most beautiful areas of the country, and its people take great pride in their environment. It is often referred to as the "Last Best Place" on account of its millions of acres of pristine, untouched wilderness. Besides tourism, their primary industries are mining, timber, service, and agriculture.

The State Motto: "EQUAL RIGHTS"

The Facts:
Wyoming became the 44th state on July 10, 1890.
Major cities: Cheyenne, Casper, Laramie, Gillette, Rock Springs
Border states: Nebraska, Colorado, Utah, Idaho, Montana, South Dakota

How Wyoming got its name:
The name Wyoming comes from an Algonquian Indian word which means "Great prairie" or "Large plains."

Fun Laws: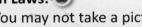
• You may not take a picture of a rabbit from January to April without an official permit.

Good to know!
• The fewest people of any US state live in Wyoming.
• It is called the Equality State because it was the first state to grant women the right to vote, in 1869. Women in other states had to wait 50 years.

OUR PRESIDENTS
OF THE UNITED STATES OF AMERICA

George Washington
1732-1799 / 1789-1797

John Adams
1735–1826 / 1797-1801

Thomas Jefferson
1743–1826 / 1801-1809

James Madison
1751–1836 / 1809-1817

James Monroe
1758–1831 / 1817-1825

John Quincy Adams
1767–1848 / 1825-1829

Andrew Jackson
1767–1845 / 1829-1837

Martin Van Buren
1782–1862 / 1837-1841

William Henry Harrison
1773–1841 / 1841-1841

John Tyler
1790–1862 / 1841-1845

James K. Polk
1795–1849 / 1845-1849

Zachary Taylor
1784–1850 / 1849-1850

Millard Fillmore
1800–1874 / 1850-1853

Franklin Pierce
1804–1869 / 1853-1857

James Buchanan
1791–1868 / 1857-1861

Abraham Lincoln
1809–1865 / 1861-1865

Andrew Johnson
1808–1875 / 1865-1869

Ulysses S. Grant
1822–1885 / 1869-1877

Rutherford B. Hayes
1822–1893 / 1877-1881

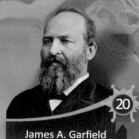

James A. Garfield
1831–1881 / 1881-1881

Chester A. Arthur
1829–1886 / 1881-1885

Grover Cleveland
1837–1908 / 1885-1889

Benjamin Harrison
1833–1901 / 1889-1893

Grover Cleveland
1837–1908 / 1893-1897

William McKinley
1843–1901 / 1897-1901

Theodore Roosevelt
1858–1919 / 1901-1909
26

William Howard Taft
1857–1930 / 1909-1913
27

Woodrow Wilson
1856–1924 / 1913-1921
28

Warren G. Harding
1865–1923 / 1921-1923
29

Calvin Coolidge
1872–1933 / 1923-1929
30

Herbert Hoover
1874–1964 / 1929-1933
31

Franklin D. Roosevelt
1882–1945 / 1933-1945
32

Harry S. Truman
1884–1972 / 1945-1953
33

Dwight D. Eisenhower
1890–1969 / 1953-1961
34

John F. Kennedy
1917–1963 / 1961-1963
35

Lyndon B. Johnson
1908–1973 / 1963-1969
36

Richard Nixon
1913–1994 / 1969-1974
37

Gerald Ford
1913–2006 / 1974-1977
38

Jimmy Carter
Born 1924 / 1977-1981
39

Ronald Reagan
1911–2004 / 1981-1989
40

George H. W. Bush
1924–2018 / 1989-1993
41

Bill Clinton
Born 1946 / 1993-2001
42

George W. Bush
Born 1946 / 2001-2009
43

Barack Obama
Born 1961 / 2009-2017
44

Donald Trump
Born 1946 / 2017...
45

Printed in Great Britain
by Amazon

44001579R10061